St Michael
Houseplants

St Michael Houseplants

Yvonne Deutch Consultant Ron Menage

Sundial

Contents

First published in 1981 by Octopus Books Limited
59 Grosvenor Street, London W1

Revised edition, 1981

© 1981 Hennerwood Publications Limited

ISBN 0 906320 18 6

Printed in England by Severn Valley Press Limited

St Michael

CHOOSING YOUR HOUSEPLANTS

The Right Plant for You

£3.15

Choosing houseplants

Houseplants bring a whole world of life and colour into the home, and they are more popular nowadays than ever before. Perhaps they re-establish the link that many city people feel that they have lost with the countryside. Undoubtedly they are very soothing, and can soften the atmosphere of a room quite remarkably. Nothing else can rival their texture, shape, colour and sheer variety, not even a painting. Plants are really more akin to sculpture, in living form.

How to choose

When you look around the horticultural department of a Marks and Spencer store, you will find a variety of plants on display. You might see one that appeals to you immediately, and decide that this is the plant for you. Before you buy it however, you should take several factors into account. The main question is whether you can provide it with the correct conditions that it needs for healthy growth. If your home is centrally heated, with a rather dry atmosphere, that delicate maidenhair fern that you liked so much in the store may literally fade away and die in your home, unless you are prepared to give it a lot of time and attention.

Care cards

To avert such tragedies, each plant is accompanied by a care card. This is plastic and triangular in shape, and has the name and picture of the plant on the front. If you turn the card over, you will find all the basic information that you need to tell you whether the plant will thrive happily in your home. You can check what temperatures it needs, whether it requires lots of light or some shade, how much water and food you should supply etc. You will also find other information, such as whether the plant needs to be provided with humid conditions, and needs spraying or pruning. If you are still in any doubt, then you should consult the assistant, who is trained to know the plants' individual growing habits, and will already have been looking after them while they are in store.

Care in the store

Marks and Spencer sell plants at peak condition, and buy the best varieties available. The horticultural department maintains a keen interest in the development of the latest varieties both in the U.K. and abroad, and are constantly testing and monitoring plants. Staff testing is just one of the excellent testing methods used. A cross section of staff who are interested in plants is chosen to monitor plants in their home environments, and each tester is supplied with a detailed form on which to enter their comments. In addition, plants are tested in the department, including ongoing comparability studies of different cultivars of the same plant.

Once in store, the plants are very carefully supervised. The staff of the horticultural sections are very well trained, and every regional office of Marks and Spencer has regular updating sessions for staff on plant care. The horticultural displays in store are carefully set up with the health of the plants in mind. You will notice that many of the plants are displayed on special capillary matting. This is made from natural fibres, with a high water retention content, and is kept moist to ensure a constant and regulated supply of water to the plants. The water provided is always tepid, since cold water can easily damage plants. The displays are kept free from draughts, correctly lit and scrupulously clean to ensure the healthiest conditions in store. Before they are put on display the plants are carefully inspected for damage and disease, and the constant cleaning of the displays not only helps aesthetically, but also prevents the build up of disease.

Packaging is of the highest quality, and every available means of protecting the plants are used – you will notice that some have plastic 'sleeves' while others are completely encased in 'floracups' which surround the plant completely to ensure maximum protection. If you choose a large plant, this will be wrapped up in a suitable manner to protect the plant from chill and physical damage on its way to your home.

Sell-by dates

Marks and Spencer have a system of ensuring that plants reach the customer in peak condition. Flowering plants have 'sell-by' dates on the pots which ensure that the plant is at its optimum growth stage when the customer takes it home, and continues to give lasting pleasure. This means that plants such as chrysanthemums are not sold when the buds are too tight. Green foliage plants are listed with a week number so that the staff can be sure that no plant remains on sale beyond its peak. This concentration on peak growth stage is also reflected in the green plant arrangements. These are specially chosen for the compatibility of the plants in any given arrangement, and the wide range of plants available means that only those in top condition at any time of the year are included in the arrangements.

Using plants well

Plants are so beautiful in themselves that you might think that as long as you put them in the right position as far as their growing needs are concerned, then all is well. To some extent this is true, however it would be a shame not to display your plants to their finest advantage. For example, if you have chosen a large plant such as a tall palm or a luscious monstera, make sure that it has enough space to make its natural impact. Climbing plants such as the *hedera* varieties, *rhoicissus* and *tradescantia* can be used in lots of ways. They can be used as room dividers, trained to climb up canes, placed on bookcases – in fact you should enhance their natural habit of reaching upwards. With trailing plants, you can exploit their habits in the opposite direction, they are excellent for decorating rooms that have very high vistas, and help to reduce the impersonality of such space. You can also play with different levels for display.

Grouping plants is not only successful from the decorative point of view, but also can be a wonderful way of ensuring their health. Choose plants which require the same growing conditions. They can create a localized micro-climate, and provide each other with vital humidity, as well as looking very luxurious and jungle-like. If your bathroom is warm and has good light, then this is a fine situation for those plants which require steamy, humid conditions, and bath time will certainly take on a new dimension, as you lie back and imagine yourself in the middle of some exotic tropical forest. As you gain in confidence and experience, you will discover many ways in which your home can be wonderfully enhanced by its green tenants.

Latin names

Throughout the book, the plants have been identified with their latin names, as well as their more common English names. Although this might seem confusing, it is in fact a method which ensures accuracy, especially since many common English names are shared by several different plants. The first part of the name is usually written with a capital letter e.g. *Philodendron*, and this refers to the genus, which literally means what kind of plant it is. Next you might have a descriptive name e.g. *Philodendron scandens*. This is not usually written with a capital letter, and is used to describe what species the plant belongs to. In this case *'scandens'* describes the climbing variety of *Philodendron*. The family from which the plant comes is indicated in brackets, e.g. *Philodendron scandens* (*Araceae*). Any extra names will indicate such things as whether the plant is variegated (*variegata*) etc. or perhaps the named cultivar, such as *Hedera helix* **'Glacier'**. These are the most general principles, remember that botany is constantly re-classifying and changing, and that the most important factor is whatever plant you have, it should always look at its best.

Your plant is carefully wrapped to ensure that it arrives home without being damaged

Healthy Houseplants

St Michael

CARING FOR YOUR PLANTS

Caring for your plants

Caring for your plant begins as soon as you have brought it home. It needs may be few, but they are vital if you are going to cultivate a thriving glossy specimen rather than a droopy straggler.

Correct light
Plants need light to carry out the process known as photosynthesis through which they make their own food supplies. Depending on the kind of plant you have, the amount of light can vary quite a lot, and it is therefore very important to know exactly what light conditions a particular plant requires for good healthy growth. Foliage plants which are all green such as the rubber plant, various ferns, umbrella plants etc should not be placed in direct light, they should be some distance away from the source of light, and sometimes in a certain amount of shade. Plants which actually enjoy some shade include the climbers and trailers, and too much light can produce yellowing of the foliage in some of these. Remember however that there are some exceptions to this general rule. For example, the variegated species must have good light because parts of their leaves are low on chlorophyll, and the green parts need the extra light to make up for this. If a variegated plant lacks light, it may loose its variegation and revert to plain green. Check on the requirements for each plant. You will notice that some of the plants sold are from the family known as Bromeliads. These are epiphytic in habit, which means that they tend to perch on the branches or in the forks of trees, or else in the shade of rocks in desert or scrub settings. There are no problems with the *cryptanthus* and the *Vriesea splendens* in the bottle garden, because the filtered light they need is supplied by the glass of the container. However, the *guzmania* in the flowering plants section will need a position in filtered sunlight. Very few plants can safely be exposed to the direct rays of hot sun, though certainly the flowering plants need excellent maximum light in order to produce good blooms. Check each plant's needs.

Temperature
As well as the provision of the appropriate light conditions, a plant must also receive properly regulated temperatures, since in general, plants that are meant to live indoors are not tolerant either of very low temperatures or wildly fluctuating extremes. In the section devoted to individual plants the ideal range of temperatures for daytime and night are supplied. Many people now have central heating, and it is therefore simple to regulate the thermostat to reflect the right temperatures. Don't worry if you can't maintain ideal temperatures, the avoidance of sudden changes should be sufficient to maintain healthy growths. One problem about central heating occurs during the winter, which is the time when plants are in their resting period. At this time they should be kept at a fairly moderate temperature, because they might struggle to continue growing, and will weaken themselves. All these factors need to be kept in mind. If you know that your home is cooler than average, then choose a plant which does not require constant warmth. (See each plant entry.) You might turn off all the heating at night, and find that the drop in temperature is so extreme that your plants drop their leaves.

Draughts
Another factor which can cause your plant to drop its leaves suddenly is the sudden influx of draughts. This basically causes a sudden and violent fluctuation in temperature, to which the plant has no defence. As well as leaf drop, the edges of the foliage may turn brown, and in the case of flowering plants, lose flowers or buds.

Watering
Ironically, one of the most common reasons for a plant's 'inexplicable' death is wrong watering procedures. You can kill a plant with too much water as with too little. Many people are surprised by this fact, because they think that extensive watering is an expression of kindness and concern for their plants. Like human beings, plants are made up of a large proportion of water, in their case, about 90%. They lose water through their leaves in the process called transpiration, by which they give off water vapour. The water is renewed by being drawn up through the roots out of the compost. If the compost is allowed to dry out, the plant is deprived of new sources of water, and in the long run it will die. Initial signs are wilting of the stems and leaves. Too much water will cause the same symptoms, and also the leaves will turn yellow. This happens because water contains oxygen, and if a constant supply is poured into the compost, the oxygen already present is displaced, and the roots literally suffocate to death, and are unable to transmit water up to the stems and leaves. Another function of water in the compost is to dissolve the substances that the plant needs for food. These are potassium and magnesium phosphates and other elements, which can only be absorbed into the roots in solution. Therefore, if your plant does not receive the right amount of water, it cannot absorb the vital nutrients that it requires to grow.

How to water
First of all, your plants do not like to be given an ice cold shower of water. It might brace you, but it can spell death for your unsuspecting plant. Tepid water is fine, and many people leave a jug of water to reach room temperature, and use it only for their plants. The technique of watering is very simple. You simply pour the water gently and steadily, allowing it to fill the space between the surface of the compost and the top of the pot. The water will seep through, and any excess will be caught in the pot holder. It is possible that the plant needs more, and you will know if this is the case because there will be no extra water in the holder. After the water has drained through, remove the excess from the holder, otherwise the roots may

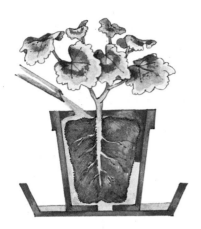

The technique of watering from above. Give enough water to fill the space between the top of the soil and the rim of the pot. The surplus should flow from the drainage holes.

If your plant has dried out completely, put the whole pot in a bucket of water so that the compost is covered. Leave it there until air bubbles stop coming to the surface.

rot. Another part of the plant that may rot if watering is not carefully carried out is the fleshy 'crown' which some plants have. The gloxinia is a good example. The crown is visible above the surface of the compost and you should be careful to water from the sides. Another option is to water from below, by pouring water into the plant holder, however this can cause the build up of substances on the surface of the compost. Perhaps the best compromise is to alternate.

Not too little

Nervous owners might try to regulate the plant's supply of water by using the 'little but often' routine, and just give the plant little trickles. This just moistens the surface of the compost, and in the meantime, the rest of the soil underneath becomes dried out. The compost shrinks away from the sides of the pot, and then all that happens when the plant is watered is that the water runs straight down the sides and out of the drainage hole at the bottom. Make sure that watering is thorough.

When to water

If your plant is wilting, and you know that you haven't supplied enough water, then there is no doubt that it needs water straight away. However, the decision about when to water on a normal basis is somewhat more complicated, and may be affected by the kind of compost in which the plant is growing. First, look at the surface of the plant. If it feels fairly moist, all should be well. Dry compost on the surface feels flaky to the touch, and will be lighter in colour than underneath. Pick up the pot and check to see if it weighs less than usual. If you have a clay pot, tap it on the side. You will hear a hollow, ringing sound rather than a solid 'clump'.

Peat composts can be very deceptive. They hold moisture longer than average, but then suddenly dry out, especially in the case of plastic containers. You have to watch carefully in case this happens, and you should also pick the pot up frequently, because when peat dries out it tends to become very light.

Do not water at the same time every day. Consult the care instructions for every plant, because they vary a great deal not only in the quantity of water that they need, but also according to the time of year and the stage of growth. A plant that is resting in the winter months for example will not appreciate the same amount of water it needs when it is producing new growth. On the other hand, during the summer months, when the plant is working overtime in its production of leaves and flowers, it needs much more water, and is losing it at a faster rate by transpiration through its foliage.

Emergency watering

A plant might accidentally dry out completely, and if this happens, you should act quickly. Fill a bucket with tepid water and plunge the pot in right over the surface of the compost. It helps to prick the dried surface with a fork to help the water to penetrate. Leave the plant submerged until you see no air bubbles coming to the surface. This will mean that the root ball has been thoroughly moistened. Lift out the plant, and let it drain for a while, before putting it back in the pot.

Soft water

Plants never mind a certain amount of acidity in the water, but there are some which positively hate lime, which causes an excess of alkaline. If you can't collect rainwater, make sure that you reduce the lime content by boiling the water first.

Humidity

Humidity is a very important feature of plant care, especially now that so many homes are centrally heated. Humidity is the amount of moisture present in the atmosphere, and because of the way plants grow, it is vital to know what level of humidity is present. Water circulates through plants by a kind of 'suction' process. As the leaves give out vapour, which is carried away in the air, a vacuum is left which encourages the plant to suck up more water through the roots. If the air is too dry, the roots cannot keep up with the pace at which the leaves are giving out water, and the plant suffers badly. The leaves dry out and wilt, and also become brown at the edges. In a properly balanced humid atmosphere, the whole process of transpiration is regulated, and the leaves will not be forced to give off so much water to the air and have to call on the roots for faster supplies.

So balance is the keynote to healthy plants.

Stand your plant in a dish of water with shingle in the middle and mist regularly to provide extra humidity.

A larger container, surrounding the one the plant is in can be packed with moist material to absorb and hold water which evaporates slowly.

How to provide humidity

If the care instructions for your plant recommend humid conditions, there are various ways in which you can supply these. You may find that you have several that enjoy humidity, and in this case, you should put them together in a group, so that they can provide their own local humidity by combining the vapour given out by their leaves in one restricted area. If a plant has to be positioned on its own, you can place it in a dish which is lined with pebbles for the pot to rest on, and fill it with water. Alternatively, put the plant in a larger container lined with peat which can be kept damp all the time. If peat is not available, you can use scrunched-up newspapers, oasis, which can be bought from florists, foam chips, polystyrene granules, anything you can think of that will hold the water for fairly long periods. Some plants enjoy the occasional steam bath, though you might be careless and use water that is too hot. Cyclamens are reputed to enjoy this experience occasionally. You simply pour warm water into a bowl, upturn another bowl so that it stands above the surface, and then rest the plant on top. The bottom of the pot should not touch the water.
In addition to the methods described above, many plants which enjoy humidity also like regular spraying or misting, especially during the warm summer months. Special sprays and misting devices can be purchased easily, and this method is particularly helpful in keeping foliage clean and free from dust, which can encourage the build up of pests and some kinds of plant diseases.
Never place a plant directly over a radiator. The atmosphere is so dry there that the plant literally shrivels to death. It is one of the most successful ways of killing a plant that you could think of.

Feeding

Plants need food to supply the energy for healthy growth, and it is not only important that they get enough food, but also the right kind. Nutrients are absorbed through the roots from the compost, and the plant uses these in all its life processes. The main elements important to plant growth are nitrogen potassium and phosphorus. Nitrogen ensures healthy growth of the leaves and shoots, but this cannot be absorbed by the plant from the air, it has to obtain it from compounds which carry the element – mainly nitrates. Every part of the plant uses phosphorus, but it is particularly valuable to the growth of new roots. Potassium is very important in flowering, and also in the production of seeds, fruits and buds.
The plant also uses various other elements which are known as 'trace elements'. These include magnesium, which helps in the production of chlorophyll, calcium, which is used to build up cell walls, also iron, sulphur, boron, molybdenum and copper. All these elements are present in very tiny amounts, yet they all combine to make up the necessary nourishment for healthy growth, and will be included in properly balanced composts.

Fertilizers

Although the above food ingredients are supplied in specially prepared compost, nitrogen, potassium and phosphorus will have to be added during the plant's growth, because these are absorbed quite rapidly. Nitrates soon dissolve away in water for example, and this is why special plant foods are available to replenish the stock as the plant feeds. The balance of these liquid fertilizers is adjusted according to whether the plant is flowering, or mainly foliage. Flowering plants need a food which has a high percentage of potassium, and not so much nitrogen, while your foliage plants will require a high content of nitrogen, and very much less potassium. When the care instructions recommend a good quality plant food, remember to buy the correct kind for flowering or foliage species. There are excellent plant foods on the market, and you should read the instructions supplied by the manufacturer for methods of dilution and quantities. Read the instructions for when to feed for the individual plant, and always feed when the compost is moist so that the food can be absorbed properly. You can tell when your plant is short of nutrients by a change in the leaf colour, but the diagnostic chart on page 22 will supply more detailed information.

Pruning and general care

Plants should be kept as well groomed as possible, not only to enhance their appearance, but also to maintain healthy conditions. Dead leaves, flowers, and straggly shoots are not only no longer useful to the plant, but can attract pests which will thrive on the decaying matter. If any stems are broken, remove them cleanly just below the damaged area. The leaves of the plant should also be kept scrupulously clean, especially those with large surfaces. These can be wiped off gently with a soft moistened cloth, and also given a wonderful gloss with one of the super new leaf shine preparations which are available in flower shops. Any dust, grit or surface spots must be removed, because the stomata through which the plant breathes can become blocked up, and also the leaf will find it hard to absorb sufficient light.

Pruning

You may find that a plant which started out with a nice bushy outline becomes very straggly, and if this happens, you will need to prune it back. This operation is usually performed at the end of winter, just before repotting, and the best policy is to cut back half of last year's new growth. This will encourage the plant to produce lots of new shoots where you want them to grow, rather than sprouting out haphazardly.

In the case of climbing plants, these can be cut back almost to the base during spring, and they also may need interim pruning in summer to keep them in control if growth is particularly vigorous. Remove the weakest and smallest shoots at this time. You can also use a technique called 'pinching back' by which you nip out the top of a shoot just above a leaf, or pair of leaves, and sometimes back to the second or third pair. By doing this, you will induce the plant to throw out more shoots lower down the stem, and so maintain a nice, bushy growth. Trailers can look particularly untidy if they are allowed to hang down with scanty growth on the stems. This is bad for the plant's health, and you should remove sections of bare stem, again to encourage new shoots further back.

Pots and containers

There is a constant debate as to whether plastic or clay containers are best for plants, but certainly the trend is for most plants to be supplied in plastic pots. These have the advantage of convenience and lightness, and are not as easy to break as the clay variety. On the other hand, they are not porous like clay pots, and may increase the danger of waterlogged plants. In fact no pot in itself can guarantee a plant's health, it is entirely up to the owner to be observant and careful. Other kinds of containers are used for plants, including window boxes, discarded sinks, old milk churns, numerous shapes and sizes of expanded polystyrene items, many with specially 'antiqued' finishes – the possibilities are endless. However, whatever container your plant is given to inhabit, it must have excellent drainage, otherwise you will end up with a mess of dank smelly roots and probably a deceased plant.

Composts

The correct compost is very important to the well being of your plant. It provides the plant's physical means of support, as well as being the medium through which it absorbs water, oxygen and vital nutrients. Plants also need different kinds of composts according to which variety they are. Some may need a preponderance of peat, others loam, but in general, a specially balanced standard compost is used. This contains proportions of sieved loam, granulated peat, some coarse river sand, fertilizer and chalk. Such a combination ensures good drainage and aeration, a supply of food which should last about three months and sufficient density to hold the correct balance of moisture.

Nowadays, there are wonderful 'space age' composts which are soil-less. They are made up from peat and sand, usually in the proportion of 3:1, plus some fertilizer. Many plants have been found to thrive particularly well in this mixture, and it is certainly excellent in terms of its lightness and convenience. One drawback however is that it is so light that it cannot support plants which have heavy top growth, or which are very tall, and these will need a weightier compost to provide sufficient anchorage.

Repotting your plants

How can you tell when your plant needs to be repotted? Do all plants need potting on every year? Do remember that every plant is different, and has individual needs. In general, you can tell when a plant is pot bound by the fact that new growth is very straggly and pale, also you may find that the root ball is wound around the soil, and that the roots themselves are growing out of the drainage holes. If you have just purchased the plant it should not need repotting the last feature described above will simply mean that the plant has been grown on capilliary matting and drew its water in this way. The plant may also be demanding an unusual amount of water. Some plants grow much faster than others, and may need to be repotted every year, while some do better if left to crowd the pot a little. The typical habits of individual plants are described in the care sections for each.

How to repot

The best time for repotting is usually in early spring, when new growth is emerging, and the plant is starting its new cycle. It would be fatal to repot during a period when the plant is resting, and not absorbing nutrients, because the richness of the new compost, and

Root growth shows a new pot is needed.

Leave 1.5–4cm between the soil and rim.

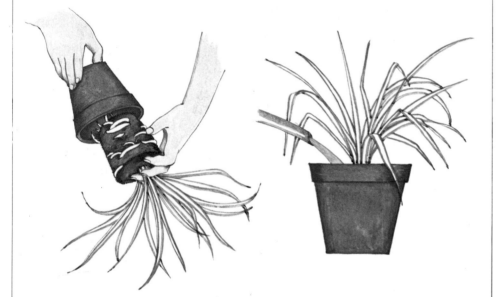

Gently remove the plant from the pot.

Tap the pot base and water at once.

Allow 1.5–2.5cm between plant and pot.

Remove cacti with a paper collar.

the amount of extra moisture available could not be used by the plant, and the new compost could become sour from underuse by the plant.

Firstly, you will have to decide on the correct size for the new pot, and a rule of thumb method is as follows. Allow 1.5–2.5cm ($\frac{1}{2}$–1in) distance between the area of the root ball and the sides of the pot. If you choose a clay pot, place a few pieces of broken clay at the bottom, which will improve drainage, and sprinkle some compost on top of these. Now remove the plant from its old pot, by turning the pot over, and gently loosening the soil ball with your fingers. The plant will slide out, and then you can trim away any straggly roots. Place the plant in the centre of the new pot, and check that there will be sufficient space at the top for watering – 1.5–4cm ($\frac{1}{2}$–1$\frac{1}{2}$in) will be adequate. Now fill the sides in with compost, gently firming it with your fingers, not your thumbs, since they will compact the soil too firmly. Just tap the surface lightly to level, and then add water. Put the plant in a warm, slightly shaded position.

Sometimes repotting into a new size pot is not necessary, but the compost may need to be renewed. In this case, tease out the old compost, spread the roots out as naturally as possible, then add the new compost, gently firming it as you proceed.

Care during holidays
Making sure that your plants receive enough water while you are away can present problems. If you have a friend who is able to 'plant-sit' for you, then you have the ideal solution. However, if this is not possible, there are various alternatives. If you have a lot of plants and they are scattered throughout the house, the best policy is to clear a space where they will all fit in order to set up a comprehensive self watering system. There are several ways of doing this. One is to stand the plants on a special water absorbent plastic matting, and allow water to drip onto the matting from a container which is situated higher

than the plants. The capillary action of the matting will draw the water through a tube leading from the container, as the roots suck in their moisture.

Another method is to pack waterholding material such as packed newspapers or peat, thoroughly saturate it, and then cover the whole lot with polythene sheeting. The 'wick' method involves the capillary system again. Buy lengths of fabric wicking or bandage, push one end into the base of the pot, and another into a bowl of water. The end that is placed in the water should be frayed out in order to increase its absorbtion capacity. If you just have a few plants, try the following methods. Water each plant well, then wrap it up, pot and all inside a transparent polythene bag, so that it creates its own micro climate. Alternatively, you can buy individual water diffusers (often sold in the shape of frogs) and place

them in individual pots. These should supply the plant with a steady supply of water for up to three weeks. Check with the supplier first to see how long they will service your plant. In every case, place the plants out of direct sunlight, because they will be forced to work harder to lose vapour through their leaves, and will use up their supplies too quickly.

If you leave your plants unattended during the winter, the supply of water is not so problematical. The danger is that they will suffer from the cold. Covering them with polythene may be the best answer here, and also remove them from situations where there is any chance of sudden draughts, such as near a window which is not double glazed.

A self-watering system can be made easily with capillary matting, a bucket and a length of tubing and a clip.

Plants that fall ill

There can be few experiences so distressing as finding that a plant that you have cared for so faithfully is failing to thrive. It may be infested with a common pest. Most living pests have one thing in mind. They are looking for a nice plant to live on, supply an endless source of free food and a built in nursery where they can have their thousands of children. Then their babies multiply themselves, and cause another cycle of problems. There are many ways in which your plants can become infected, but the main point is to know what to do about it.

Listen to your plants
Firstly, keep your eyes open. Many people believe that because they talk regularly to their plants and encourage them with uplifting chats, then they will have no problems. However, this may prevent your plants from talking to you. You may be so preoccupied with talking to them, that you are not listening to what they are saying. Plant language is transmitted through the leaves, stems and flowers, and the diagnostic chart on page 22 will help you to translate what is being communicated.

Early warning signals
The diagnostic chart really indicates conditions that are already well advanced, and it might be too late in some cases for treatment to work. The best policy is to learn to take notice of any small changes that occur, and it will help if you read through the list of symptoms and causes to 'memorize' the kinds of clues that tell you something is going wrong. Although insecticides are very effective, you can do a lot through taking preventive measures. Examine foliage regularly for discolouration, any furriness, patchiness etc. Also check stems, roots and flowers. Remember to check on the underside of leaves, and in any hidden crevices, since some pests hide themselves very cleverly.

A very useful item in helping you to examine your houseplants is an inexpensive magnifying glass, since many pests are tiny, and cannot be seen with the naked eye. Regular spraying and cleaning of foliage is an invaluable part of a plant health routine, since this prevents the build up of dust and decaying matter which attracts predators. As you begin to develop this automatic routine, you will acquire a 'feel' for the condition of your plants, and you will sense when all is not well.

Using insecticides

The more warnings we receive about the way that insecticides affect our environment, the more careful and responsible we should be about using them. They should really be used as the last resort, because if you are following a regular checking routine, you will be able to spot infestations early enough to deal with them without engaging in a domestic version of chemical warfare. Early attacks can be dealt with by less drastic methods. Larger pests like mealy bugs can be picked off with tweezers, while others can be swabbed off with cotton wool soaked in methylated spirit. Cotton wool tipped sticks can be used to clean awkward areas. Another method is to wash the infestation off with a detergent solution, which you should then rinse off with clear water.

If you are unlucky enough to have a plant that is really badly infested, and needs chemical treatment, remember that insecticides should be used with care. Close off the room in which you are working, remove children and pets, cover fish tanks if they are non-portable, and open a window. Follow the manufacturer's instructions to the letter. Always take care with the storage of insecticides, especially when there are children about. They should be clearly labelled, kept in their own containers (not in old squash bottles which might attract a child) and most important, they should be kept in a securely locked place. The cupboard where you lock up other dangerous materials is ideal.

Diseases

Unlike insect pests, diseases such as rusts, moulds and mildews do not come looking for your plants. They are inevitably caused by poor growing conditions. If a plant is pot bound, the roots may begin to rot, and if the atmosphere is damp and insufficiently ventilated, the plant may become mildewed. If you spot the symptoms quickly enough, and change the growing conditions early, then the plant will have a good chance of recovering by itself. Any infected parts should be removed immediately however, because they will spread the disease further. Regular cleaning of the plant will help to prevent diseases, and it should always be sprayed with a fungicide if it has had to spend any time outdoors.

Growing pains

There is something very dramatic in discussing the various kinds of pests and diseases, but the truth is that most plants get into difficulties in a much more prosaic manner – simply because of the way that they are cultivated. Many plants die because their owners fail to supply the correct light, humidity, food, water, and many other conditions. In fact your plants may succumb to pests and diseases only because they are not grown in a healthy manner to begin with.

Watering

Some people literally drown their plants by giving them too much water, others seem to think that they are capable of walking to the tap and getting a drink for themselves. Failure to water a plant in the correct manner can cause severe problems, and it is therefore vital that you follow the instructions given for individual specimens.

The symptoms of incorrect watering are the same whether your plant gets too much or too little. The plant wilts, the leaves become dehydrated, and start to drop. All this means that it is failing to absorb water properly. If the plant is too dry, the compost is crumbly and arid, and if the plant is waterlogged, then the roots are badly affected, and are unable to take in water. It is easy to diagnose the first condition, but with over watering, the damage is happening out of sight.

The over watered plant is basically being suffocated. A properly moist compost also contains air, and if too much water is poured on to an already damp medium, it displaces the air already present. As a consequence the roots are deprived of vital oxygen, and suffocate. Eventually they die, and the rest of the plant dies too.

If your plant shows signs of distress from over watering, it can be removed from the pot and allowed to dry out. It can then be replaced and watered with a Benomyl solution which inhibits the growth of fungi.

Sun scald

Sun scald is caused by plants being placed in direct sunlight when in fact they need protection. This condition can be enhanced when the sun is shining through spots of water left on the leaves, which act as magnifying glasses, and focus the heat. Damage will be in the form of dried out areas on the foliage – they look like what they in fact are – burns.

Cold water scorch

Some plants like gloxinias hate cold water on their leaves. Distinctive marbled patches are present, rather like the effects of leaf miners (see page 20). Always use tepid water, and avoid leaving drops on the foliage.

Physical damage

Plants should never be handled roughly, but if this has happened, the symptoms are very evident. There may be holes or tears in the leaves, or, if the growing tip has been knocked badly, the ensuing leaves will be distorted and possibly stunted. This often happens to plants which are positioned in a multi-traffic area like a hall. People pass by and knock the plant with coats, umbrellas, cricket bats, tennis racquets et al, and the poor plant literally doesn't have a chance to recover. If the initial damage is minimal, the plant will grow new parts eventually, but you cannot expect a plant to defend itself against constant assault.

Draughts

The most common plant reaction to draughts, especially if they are delicate species, is to drop their leaves suddenly and dramatically. Sturdier varieties may simply droop a little, but if either reaction occurs, the plant must be moved to a protected spot.

Changes in temperature

In the sections on the individual plants, two sets of temperatures are supplied, one for day, and one for night. Since many people have central heating and can regulate their temperatures, the damage caused by uncontrolled fluctuation can be prevented. The problems usually arise more from the sudden difference in temperature than a very low one – the sudden change causes rapid leaf drop, in some cases overnight. Very few plants can tolerate being placed on a windowsill in direct sun, but even those that can may suffer if the temperature drops very severely. It is better to keep plants where they are more assured of consistent temperature conditions.

Humidity

This is as important a feature of care for some plants as correct watering and feeding. Many species come from warm, moist climates, and require steady heat and ample moisture in the air. The symptoms are browning of the tips and the edges of foliage. Supply good humidity in the manner described on page 14.

Aerosol sprays

Our homes are full of wonder sprays for polishing furniture, freshening air, setting hair etc. Some can damage leaves by building up a film on the surface, or by producing tiny specks, and any deposits should be washed off regularly.

Spray a thin mist of water into the air above the plants for extra humidity.

Pests

Ants These are not only a general nuisance in the home, but can also affect your plants by loosening the soil in pots, and carrying aphids from one plant to another.
Treatment Sprinkle drops of Panant close to the pots.

Aphids Look for aphids in spring and summer. Also known as greenfly and plant lice, these are very fast spreading pests, and are rapidly developing resistance to insecticides. They are tiny green creatures about 2mm ($\frac{1}{8}$in) long, and sometimes have wings. Aphids stab into the plant tissue with their needle sharp mouthparts, and feed on the sap. They cluster on the tips of new shoots and on the underside of leaves. The plant's growth is distorted and inhibited, causing the leaves to curl and turn yellow. The insects secrete a sticky substance called honeydew, which encourages the growth of a black fungus called sooty mould. (The combination of honeydew and sooty mould is caused by other insect pests too).
Treatment The aphids can be sprayed with Derris or Malathion, and the sooty mould can be washed off with a mild detergent solution. Rinse off with clear water afterwards.

Caterpillars These might appear on plants which have spent a period outdoors, or those in hanging baskets. The caterpillars chew holes in the leaves.
Treatment Pick off the caterpillars by hand.

Leaf miners In adult form, the leaf miner is a tiny fly. However it is the maggot that causes the damage. The fly lays its eggs on the leaves, and as the maggot hatches it feeds on the leaf tissue just below the surface, and stays there, moving as it feeds. You will see pale brown or light green wavy lines which follow the maggot's path, also blisters appear on the leaf, and can completely cover the surface. Plants most frequently attacked are chrysanthemums and cinerarias, but others can be infested too.
Treatment Cut away affected leaves, and spray with Malathion.

Mealy bugs These appear in the summer, and look like blobs of white fluff. In fact they are dark grey insects, which collect in stationary masses mainly in the joints of stems, or in the crevices of the necks of bulbs such as the hippeastrum. They may also appear on the undersides of leaves, near the veins. The young are incubated in the fluff, and are flattish blobs of pale brown or yellow. They have no protective woolly coat.
Treatment Scrape off the most accessible bugs with the back of a knife, then spray with Malathion, once a week for three weeks. Alternatively, use a swab of cotton wool dipped in methylated spirit (a cotton bud is ideal).

Red spider mite This pest thrives in hot, dry conditions such as centrally heated air. They are so minute that they are visible only wih a magnifying glass, but their damage is very evident. The mites are pale yellow or red, round in shape, and suck up the sap, casting off their skins as they thrive, leaving them stuck all over the leaf. They also produce a matted webbing, which wraps around stems.
Good humidity and watering should protect the plant, which can otherwise be choked and mottled all over in a bad attack.
Treatment Spray with liquid Derris twice a week for three weeks.

Root mealy bugs These are like fat little white woodlice, which live in the roots and compost. They can seriously inhibit the growth of the plant.
Treatment Remove the plant and shake off the soil from the roots. Wash the remaining soil and bugs away, then repot in new compost. Water the compost with a solution of Malathion once a week for two weeks.

Left: Aphids feed on the young growths of plants. **Below:** Check carefully for root mealy bugs.

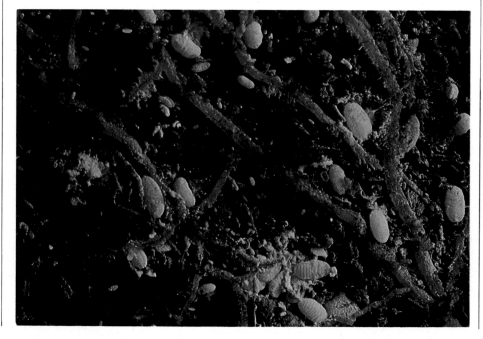

Scale insects You will see clusters of small, immobile waxy shells on the stems or bark of the plant. These are the protective covers for the eggs, which grow under the scales, and feed on the sap. They then grow up and find their own patch, and make more shells. These gradually enlarge and become pale green, and as the insects feed, they exude lots of sticky honeydew, which breeds sooty mould.

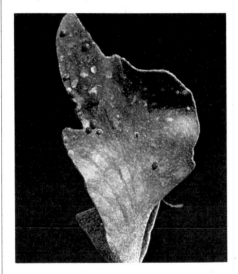

Treatment Rub off the scales with a cotton wool swab dipped in methylated spirit, or scrape off gently with the back of a knife onto a sheet of paper beneath, and spray with Malathion, repeating twice more at ten day intervals.

Sciarid fly This is an annoying pest which breeds its larvae in the potting compost. Once the adults emerge, they fly up on the plant. The larvae feed on decaying organic matter in the soil, and may nibble on the roots. They are white with a black head, and though small, they can be seen with the naked eye.
Treatment Water the compost with a Malathion solution once a week for two weeks.

Slugs and snails These may attack plants that are put outdoors for a period. You will see a slimy trail, and bitten foliage. They hide during the day, look under the pot or under the foliage.
Treatment Remove by hand.

Thrips These are tiny black winged insects which attack leaves and flowers, producing white dots and streaks. They might attack flower buds badly enough to prevent flowering, but infestations are very uncommon.
Treatment Spray with Malathion once a week for two weeks.

White fly This is a tiny, white moth-like creature which collects on the underside of leaves. The damage is caused by the larvae, which look like round, transparent scales sticking to the leaf. They suck out the sap, and produce lots of honeydew, which causes the leaves to turn a messy grey. In bad attacks the plant can die.
Treatment Cut off infected parts, and spray the plant several times at intervals of three to four days with Bioresmethrin, which destroys the larvae. Eventually the adults die off naturally.

Left: Scale insects. **Right:** White fly. **Below:** Botrytis.

Diseases

Botrytis (grey mould) This is a fungus, and lives on old leaves and flowers discarded by the plant. Under cool, moist conditions, it starts to thrive, and attacks the living plant. It starts off as brown patches on the leaves, which then produces a fluffy grey fur. Cyclamen and gloxinia are very prone to this disease.
Treatment Cut off the affected parts and spray with Benomyl once a week for three weeks.

Fungal spots These appear as soft brown roughly circular patches on the leaf. Humid conditions might encourage them, and the plants most susceptible are dracaenas, hedera and dieffenbachia. The disease is not common, and not major in effect, but it can spoil the look of the plant.

Treatment Spray once a week with Benomyl for three weeks. Badly affected leaves should be removed, otherwise leave intact.

Above: Fungal spot.

Mildew This appears in two forms, either powdery or downy. Powdery mildew looks like white dust on the leaf, while the downy kind is fluffy. It mainly appears in the summer, when plants are dry at the roots, and very warm. Poor air circulation can also cause mildew. Begonias and chrysanthemums are very prone to attack. Prevent by dusting lightly every other week with Sulphur or Thiram.

Treatment If plants are not protected regularly, and outbreaks have occurred, dust twice a week with Sulphur or Thiram.

Below: Mildew.

Diagnostic chart

Leaf symptoms	Causes
Base leaves turn yellow and fall off.	Excess water in compost. Remove from container for one day to dry out. Do not water for several days.
Base leaves turn yellow, but do not drop.	Sudden cold or drop in normal temperature. Check temperature.
Yellow mottling, rings or streaks appear. Plant is slow to grow and stunted.	Virus infection spread by greenfly and other sucking insects. Destroy infected plant immediately.
Yellow specks and web on leaf or stems.	Red spider mite. See page 20.
Leaves are pale green, turning yellow. Plant is straggly, not growing well.	Insufficient nitrogen. Supply food with higher nitrogen content, repot plant, or supply more light.
Leaves lose variegation and revert to green.	If all leaves are green, plant needs more light. If one branch only is green, reversion is occurring. Remove affected shoots.
Coloured leaves fade or revert.	Insufficient light. Compost too wet.
Edges and tips of leaves turn brown.	Atmosphere may be too dry. Check for draughts, also lime in water or compost. Perhaps a lack of potash.
Leaves have brown spots.	Cold, if plant is succulent; dry fertilizer on leaves; over feeding; sun shining through water left on leaves; gas fumes; wrongly balanced compost.
Hard brown or pale yellow spots on leaf.	Scale insects. See page 21.
Large brown patches on leaves, becoming papery.	Too much direct sun.
Wavy lines and blisters on leaf surface.	Leaf miner. See page 20.
Furry white markings on leaves, marbled effect.	Cold water on leaves; watering with cold rather than tepid water. Especially affects gloxinias.
Powdery white patches all over plant.	Powdery mildew. See page 22.
Small, furry white spots on stems and leaf joints.	Mealy bugs. See page 20.
Furry grey patches on leaves, also brown and yellow marks.	Grey mould. See page 21.
Azalea leaves have thickened leaves and grey covering.	Azalea gall fungus. See page 23.
Leaves look greyish. New growth is poor. Leaves are falling.	Red spider mite. See page 20. (Effect varies with different plants).

Leaf symptoms	Causes
Plant wilting, leaves hanging limply.	Compost too dry or too set. If too wet remove from pot and dry out. Do not water for several days. Otherwise, supply more water.
Leaves curl and look distorted. Sometimes turn yellow.	Check for greenfly or scale insects. See pages 20–21.
Sooty black patches on leaves.	Sooty mould. Could be scale insect, green fly or white fly. See pages 20–21.
Leaves covered with sticky patches.	Honeydew from scale insects, green fly or white fly. See pages 20–21.
Leaves have large holes.	Slugs, snails or caterpillars. See pages 20–21.
Fleshy leaves are turning brown at soil level	Excess water and/or temperature too low. Stop watering for a few days.
Leaves falling. No change in colour.	Sudden drop in temperature or cold draught. Change position, or check temperature.

Symptoms on rest of plant	Causes
Premature falling of flowers. Bud drop.	Draughts; dry atmosphere; cold; over or under watering; too little sun; moving plant; red spider mite. See page 20. Maintain correct care procedures for plant.
Plant fails to flower.	Too little nourishment and light; if very lush and leafy, too much nitrogen; posssibly not enough warmth. Supply high potash feed, increase humidity.
Hyacinth flowers brown, or spike discoloured and stunted.	Insufficient water when bulbs were in darkness.
Flowers failing to set fruit.	Air too dry; not enough food, especially potash; compost too dry.
Badly shaped fruit.	Dry atmosphere during pollination.
Fruit shrivels or falls.	Too little water; atmosphere too hot and dry.
Raised hard spots, brown, grey or black on bark and branches. Plant not thriving.	Scale insects. See page 21.
Fluffy white spots on stems, also inside neck of bulbs, especially hippeastrum.	Mealy bugs. See page 20.
Brown rot on stems at soil level; also on crowns of complete plants. Grey fur growing after.	Cold conditions plus over-watering, leading to grey mould. See page 21.

Root disease and damping off This is caused by unsterile soil and moist cool conditions. The plant wilts while the soil is still moist and the roots and stems may rot.
Treatment Repot in new compost if necessary, and check cultivating conditions for too much moisture or too cool a temperature. Water compost with Benomyl solution once every ten days for three weeks.

Above: Root disease and damping off.

Rust and azalea gall Rust appears as raised reddish brown powdery spots on the underside of the leaf, and azalea gall results in thick, blistered leaves, which become grey white in colour. The flowers may also be discoloured.
Treatment Remove infected parts, and spray twice a week with Thiram.

Sooty mould This is the black fungus which breeds on the honeydew exuded by various insect pests. It does not harm the plant itself, but combined with the honeydew it can block the stomata and hinder transpiration. It also collects dust.
Treatment Treat the pest according to which kind it is, and wipe off the mould with a solution of mild detergent. Rinse off with clear water afterwards.

The Indoor Flower Garden

St Michael

FLOWERING PLANTS

Aphelandra squarrosa
(Acanthaceae)
Saffron spike, Zebra plant.

This is a very attractive and unusual houseplant, and its common names are easily explained by its bright yellow spike and elegantly striped foliage. *Aphelandra* comes from Brazil, and the cultivar sold is called **'Dania'**. This is a compact variety of *A.squarrosa*, and has pleasing, silvery striped leaves. It grows to about 30cm (1ft), and was a great favourite with the Victorians who grew it in conservatories. The plant has a distinctive spiky central bract, which appears in the winter. The flowers emerge from this in plume like clusters and last about six weeks between April and August. The plant likes plenty of warmth and humidity, and the minimum temperature at which it will over-winter is 10°C (50°F).

Care

Temperature
21°–24°C (70°–75°F) Day
16°–18°C (60°–65°F) Night

Position: Place in maximum natural light, and avoid draughts or the leaves may drop. Keep out of direct sunlight.

Watering: Water every day and keep the plant permanently moist, since it has lots of roots.

Feeding: Feed once a week during summer and early autumn with a good quality plant food.

Extra care: Provide good humidity by placing the pot in a tray lined with pebbles and filled with water, or else place it in a larger container which is lined with peat which can be kept moistened. Spray often during hot weather.
Aphelandra can be cut back to promote growth for the following year. To do this, wait till the flowers die off, then cut off the spike along with one or two pairs of leaves to just above the next pair.

Carry on watering, and the plant will produce side shoots lower down. Over winter the plant at the recommended minimum winter temperature, and the bract will grow again. The plant can be repotted in a loam based compost.

Flowering time: Bract in early winter, and flowers for six weeks between April and August.

Azalea simsii
syn Rhododendron simsii
(Ericaceae)

In the language of flowers, the azalea is supposed to convey the meaning 'temperance', however nothing could be further from the mood of this delightful plant with its deliciously frivolous delicately frilled blooms. The traditional meaning was applied to remind frivolous people to tone themselves down perhaps. The flowers can be red, pink, white, or multicoloured combinations, and appear in late winter or early spring. They are 2.5–10cm (1–4in) across. The foliage is neat and compact with evergreen leaves, and last from two to four weeks, and the plant usually grows around 15–60cm (6–24in) in height. The hybrids seen nowadays are bred from the Japanese *R.indicum* and *R.simsii*, which comes from China.
Azaleas have a reputation for being somewhat difficult to care for. They need lime free water for example, and do not like dry, stuffy atmospheres, which will cause them to drop their leaves. They enjoy some humidity, but not too

much warmth, and the leaves should always be misted, rather than sprayed.

Care

Temperature
13°–16°C (55°–60°F) Day
4°–13°C (40°–55°F) Night

Position: Place in good natural light, out of direct draughts, but with plenty of air.

Watering: Use lime free water (boil first, then cool). The plant should be watered daily while in flower. To tell how much it needs, look at the main stem. This will have a ring or water mark, the higher the mark, the less water it needs. If there is no mark, feel the pot to check if it is light. If it is, the pot should be plunged into a bucket of tepid water to cover the compost.

Feeding Feed once a week in summer, but only during the bud stage. Stop feeding then until flowering is over.

Extra care: Provide some humidity, and mist the plant during hot weather. Do not spray or you will damage the petals. After flowering is over, cut the shoots back by about $\frac{1}{8}$th of their length. Clip above any side shoots, and provide water to encourage new shoots. The plant can be repotted in a slightly acid peat based compost, and will enjoy being placed out in the garden from June to September. Sink the pot into the soil in a sunny position, and feed every two weeks.

Provide water regularly, and bring indoors when the weather begins to get cooler. Stop feeding, and water sparingly. Place in a temperature of about 16°C (60°F) to encourage new buds to form. Once they are growing, resume normal watering.

Flowering time: Early winter or late spring, for two to four weeks.

Begonia
(Begoniaceae)

Begonias are named after Michel Begon (1638–1710) who was a French administrator and a very enthusiastic amateur botanist. He was posted to the French Antilles in 1681, and brought back samples of begonias to Europe. He had a large collection of illustrated botanical books which he made available to other interested botanists. Other varieties of begonia have been found throughout the tropics and sub tropics, some with exquisite foliage, others with a wide range of flower types.

Begonias dislike stuffy dry conditions, and prefer lots of humidity. The wrong conditions will cause mildew, and so will water left on their leaves. The cultivars sold are chosen from a special long lasting strain, and produce small clusters of flowers from the leaf axils.

Begonias are grown in small rooting containers within the pots. This in no way restricts the growth of the plant.

'Elfe' is a double bloom of compact size in a delicate pale pink, shading to deeper pink.

'Sirene' has a similar flower, in a deep, true red.

'Ballerina' is one of the most recent introductions, and caused much excitement when it was first shown at the Chelsea Flower Show. The flower is slightly larger and denser than **'Elfe'** and **'Sirene'**, and has a lovely orange colour.

'Balalaika' and **'Mandela'** have the same flower size and shape as **'Ballerina'**, and are yellow, a shade deeper than primrose.

Care

Temperature
20°–22°C (68°–72°F) Day
10°–13°C (50°–55°F) Night

Position: Good natural light, but not in direct sunlight. Keep away from draughts, but provide some ventilation.

Watering: Water just enough to keep the compost moist all the time. Do not water the leaves.

Feeding: Feed once a week during flowering with a dilute solution of good quality plant food.

The variety of Begonia available may vary from store to store but will be selected from the above.

Extra care: Remove any dead flowers regularly, and check for signs of mildew. To increase the length of the flowering period, you will need to maintain steady warmth and lots of humidity. Keep at normal temperatures and either stand the pot in a tray lined with pebbles and filled with water, or else put it in a larger container lined with peat which can be kept moist. These begonias can be grown out of doors, but not until danger of frost is passed.

Kalanchoë blossfeldiana
(Crassulaceae)
Flaming Katy

The Kalanchoe makes a welcome splash of colour during the winter months, with its masses of tiny bright red or orange flowers perched on its shiny green foliage. It is a succulent plant and comes from Madagascar. The leaves have a waxy texture and are about 2.5–5cm (1–2in) long. This is a good compact little plant, which grows about 20–30cm (8–12in) high, and is very easy to care for. The flowers are long lasting too, they bloom for several weeks in the winter months, and need some humidity to obtain the best results. The cultivars sold are **'Blossfeldiana'** hybrids, **'Annette'** and **'Christine'**.

Care

Temperature
20°–22°C (68°–72°F) Day
10°–16°C (50°60°F) Night

Position: Provide maximum natural light in winter and keep out of draughts. In summer provide some shade.

Watering: Water with tepid water when the compost feels dry. Do not let the roots stand in excess water in the potholder.

Feeding: Feed once a week during the summer with a good quality plant food. Stop feeding during winter when the plants start to flower.

Extra care: Remove dead flowers regularly. After flowering is over cut back the stem to one pair of leaves and repot in a soil based compost with some grit added. When the plant starts growing, water and start feeding until flowers appear. Continue water and stop food.

Flowering time: About six to eight weeks during winter months.

Hydrangea macrophylla
(Hydrangeaceae)

Hydrangeas are really showy pot plants, and are very fascinating in the way that they can adapt their colour depending on the amount of acid in the soil. The plant originates in Japan and North America, and is usually bought as a pot specimen when it is about 45–60cm (18–24in) tall. Hydrangea is basically a hardy shrub, with shiny oval leaves and large flower heads. These are clusters of individual blooms, which are about 20–25cm (8–10in) in diameter. The individual florets are about 2.5cm (1in) across. The clusters are made up of groups of male and female florets, some fertile some not. The infertile ones are the most showy. The colour of the blooms can be regulated by control of the acidity of the soil, so that shades of deep blue, vivid purple, red, soft pink, pale blue and even white can be achieved. Acid soil produces the most intense blue flowers, and this can be heightened by adding alum or special colouring agents which can be bought. Lime rich soil influences the red to pink shades, but it is a mistake to try to change a blue flower to a red one, you will only get a muddy yellow effect. The plant blooms in spring. The flowers last about six weeks. In the language of flowers, the hydrangea represents 'A boaster', or 'Heartless'.
It can also be grown successfully out of doors.

Care

Temperature
16°–18°C (60°–65°F) Day
13°–16°C (55°–60°F) Night

Position: Choose a spot with maximum natural light, but out of direct sunlight. Avoid draughts.

Watering: Water frequently and keep the compost moist at all times. Use soft water, especially for the blue flowered varieties.

Feeding: Feed once a week with a good quality plant food.

Extra care: The plant can be planted outside after flowering is over. Watch out for aphids.

Flowering time: Flowers bloom for 6 weeks.

Pelargonium
(Geraniaceae)
Geranium, Storksbill

Legend has it that once the prophet Mohammed washed his shirt and hung it to dry on a mallow plant. When he returned to retrieve his shirt, the plant had turned into a beautiful geranium. Whatever its legendary associations, the geranium family is certainly one of the most well loved houseplants. They have graced the homes of rich and poor for generations, and have been grown not only for their undeniable attractiveness as flowers, but also for their useful leaves. These are soft and plush, often with conspicuous zonal markings. Some are very beautifully scented, and have been crushed to extract their oils for toilet waters and cosmetics. If you grew a garden full of different kinds, you would find all sorts of fragrances and flavours – apples, roses, mint, orange, nutmeg, lemon, almond, apricot, lavender – all these from the familiar geranium. Many delicate puddings and delicious jams and jellies get their flavours from the leaves. The plant originates from South Africa, and has its common name because its seed is shaped like the stork's beak. In the language of flowers, the dark geranium represents melancholy, the scarlet geranium, comfort. Varieties sold are the Regal or show kinds, which have large, showy flowers. The Slam varieties include **'Grand Slam'** which is deep rose pink and violet, and **'Lavender Grand Slam'** in mauve and maroon. A range of F¹ hybrids are sold only as bedding plants. Pelargoniums dislike hot stuffy rooms, and should be given an airy situation.

Care

Temperature
20°–22°C (68°–72°F) Day
10°–13°C (50°–55°F) Night

Position: Place in maximum natural light, away from draughts.

Watering: Water frequently, and never let the compost dry out.

Feeding: Feed once a week from April to September with a good quality plant food.

Extra care: Remove any dead flowers regularly. The plant can be placed outdoors in the garden between June and September. Keep the plant cool at 7°C (45°F) and rather dry in winter. They can be repotted every spring with a general purpose potting medium.

Flowering times: For one month in late spring to early summer.

Hyacinthus
(Liliaceae)
Hyacinth

A bowl of hyacinths makes a fragrant addition to the household during Christmas and the New Year. The cultivars sold are shades of pink, blue and white. Specially prepared bulbs are used for early flowering, and are sold coming into flower. The plant is about 30cm (12in) high, with narrow, glossy, strap-like leaves, and a dense cluster of bell shaped, waxy-textured flowers. These have a delightful scent which can pervade a closed room, and last for several weeks after the flowers have emerged. In the language of flowers, the plant means 'sport', 'game' or 'play'. The hyacinth is reputedly named after a Greek prince called Hyakinthos, who was killed by Zephyrus, the god of the West wind. The flower grew from the blood of the murdered prince.

Care

Temperature
13°–16°C (55°–66°F) Day
 4°–10°C (40°–50°F) Night

Position: Place in maximum light, well protected from draughts.

Watering: Keep the compost well moistened, but not waterlogged.

Feeding: Feeding is not needed.

Extra care: Bulbs specially prepared for early flowering cannot be used again. Plant unprepared bulbs outdoors in autumn for spring flowering.

Flowering time: About two weeks after flowers have opened.

Saintpaulia ionantha
(Gesneriaceae)
African Violet

The Saintpaulia is one of the most popular of flowering houseplants. The original species was found in the mountains of Tanzania in East Africa. Its flowers are similar in shape to those of a broad-petalled violet, hence its common name. Modern breeding methods have produced beautifully coloured forms in pink, purple, magenta and blue as well as blue-violet forms. Some produce single blooms, some double or frilly petalled. The leaves are round and heart-shaped at the base, usually dark and velvety. The varieties sold are **'Ada'**, **'Afra'**, **'Alea'**, **'Annette'**, **'Antje'**, **'Bine'**, **'Candy'** and **'Richarda'**.

Care

Temperature
13°–21°C (55°–70°F) Day
10°–16°C (50°–60°F) Night

Position: Place in maximum natural light and avoid draughts or the leaves may drop. Keep out of direct sunlight.

Watering: Water when the compost feels slightly dry. Add tepid water slowly until it drains into the pot holder.

Feeding: Feed once a week with a good quality plant food, from April until September.

Extra Care: Water very carefully, never allowing the compost to become soaked and make sure that the water does not drop onto the leaves. African violets are especially prone to sun scald, which results in large brown patches on the leaves which may become papery so avoiding direct sunlight is essential. Humidity is also important and some shingle or pebbles in a pot holder or container which will retain water will provide the humidity a hairy leaved plant requires. Do not mist.

Flowering time: The most.

blooms are produced in summer but with care it will produce some blooms throughout the year.

Orchids
(Orchidaceae)

Tropical orchids were relatively unknown in the western world until the 18th century. Many famous names are associated with their introduction, notably Charles Darwin and Captain Cook. During the 19th century interest blossomed and their cultivation became a favourite Victorian horticultural hobby. It was not until much later that the potential of cymbidium hybrids was realised. Today they are the most popular orchids in cultivation. These lovely blooms are on sale in Marks and Spencer as cut flowers in three forms. The Boxed Cymbidium is a single bloom attractively packaged with the stem in its own bottle of preservative. This makes a lovely gift or attractive table decoration which your guests could take home with them as a parting gift. The mini *Cymbidium* and *Cymbidium* spray are displayed

Far left: *Saintpaulia ionantha*, African
Violet. **Left:** *Aranda* 'Christine'. **Above:**
Dendrobium 'Pure White' and
'Madame Pompadour'. **Right:**
Cymbidium spray.

best as single stem arrangements.
They are sold with the cut end of
the stem encased in its own water
holder.

The other orchids sold in Marks
and Spencer are the *Dendrobium*
and *Aranda* which are flown in
from the Far East. The main
varieties sold are *Dendrobium*
'Madame Pompadour' and
'Pure White' and *Aranda*
'Christine' (speckled pink). These
are sold with three stems in a
bunch, some with foliage for
display.

Care

Temperature: Orchids will keep
best at 10°–16°C (50°–60°F)

1. Always use clean water and
vase.
2. Cut at least half an inch off
stems with a sharp knife.
3. Change water and recut stems
every 4 days.

Flowering time: Orchids are
easy flowers to look after and
should last for at least a week
after purchase.

Campanula isophylla
(Campanulaceae)
Italian bellflower

This delightful flowering plant comes from northern Italy, where it is trailing in habit with purple bell shaped flowers, opening into star formations. They are about 2.5cm (1in) wide and flower from mid summer to late autumn. They look very pretty in hanging baskets, and also come in blue and white forms. We also have our own wild variety of campanula, including the trailing ivy leaved kind which is known as Witches' thimbles in Somerset. Another close relative is the harebell, for which local names abound. It is called Fairy cap in Wiltshire, Fairy bells, Fairy thimble and Lady's thimble in Somerset, and Cuckoos in Devon. There are various taboos about picking the flower because of its alleged ownership by the fairies who will punish or enchant you if you steal the flower.

As a houseplant, *C. isophylla* is extremely easy to care for, and simply requires good light and plenty of room to trail. In the language of flowers, the plant means 'Constance' or 'Gratitude'

Care

Temperature
20°–22°C (68°–72°F) Day
10°–13°C (50°–55°F) Night

Position: Maximum natural light, but not in direct sunlight. Avoid draughts and sudden chills.

Watering: Water when compost is slightly dry, and do not let the roots stand in excess water in the potholder. Water more sparingly during winter.

Feeding: Feed once a week during flowering with a good quality plant food.

Extra care: Remove dead flowers regularly. After flowering is over, cut back the stems to points where new leaves and shoots appear. Keep fairly cool over winter, about

10°C (50°F). Repot when necessary in a peat based compost.

Flowering time: Flowers continuously from early summer to late autumn. Can be grown outdoors after danger of frosts.

Fuchsia
(Onagraceae)
Lady's Eardrops

With their unusual and highly attractive flowers, fuchsias make delightful pot plants, and are especially suitable for a fairly cool room which does not have central heating. They were very popular plants in Victorian conservatories, and have regained their status to the extent that there are specialist

Front: *Campanula isophylla*, Italian bellflower. **Back:** The lovely Fuchsia.

fuchsia societies which attract thousands of enthusiasts. Originally from Central and South America and New Zealand, the species was named after the sixteenth century German botanist Leonhart Fuchs. The cultivars sold by Marks and Spencer are mostly upright in habit, though there are of course many trailing varieties. The distinctive flower looks exactly like the common name suggests – a very glamourous drop-type earring. The centre is tubular, and is surrounded by pointed petals which bend backwards when the flower is fully opened. From the centre of the tube hangs a cascade of pretty stamens. The individual flowers are usually about 7.5cm

$(1\frac{1}{2}$in) long, and the leaves are oval shaped. The plants start flowering from mid-April through to August, depending on the cultivar, and flowering continues right up till Autumn. Although the cultivars are able to tolerate fairly cool conditions, none are hardy. They can be placed outdoors through June to September however, when there is no danger from frost. In fact many people believe that a period outside is positively beneficial to fuchsias, but do remember never to move them at all when they are in bud, since the buds are delicate and might drop. In the language of flowers the fuchsia means 'Taste'. Cultivars are sold from the following selection, though not all of them may be available in a particular store at any given time:

'Beacon', 'Display', 'Dollar Princess' (all red colours)
'Peppermint Stick' (Pink and mauve)
'Winston Churchill' (Reddish mauve, shorter in habit than others)
'Pink Spangles' (Pink).

Care

Temperature
13°–16°C (55°–60°F) Day
  4°–10°C (40°–50°F) Night

Position: Keep in the best possible natural light, but avoid direct sunlight. Keep the plant protected from draughts.

Watering: Watering should be frequent and regular – the compost must never be allowed to dry out completely. Do not let the plant become waterlogged however, just make sure the compost is always moist. Use tepid water, and pour slowly until it drains into the pot holder. Remove excess water from the pot holder.

Feeding: Feed once a week from April to September with a good quality plant food.

Extra care: Remove dead flowers regularly. After flowering is over, reduce the amount of water

supplied, and cut back to the strongest stems. Keep out of frosts during winter, and supply just enough water to keep the compost barely moist. When new shoots appear in the spring, cut back further if necessary, to keep the plant bushy and upright. Avoid erratic watering, which may cause both the leaves and flowers to drop. The most common pests to look out for are aphids, whitefly and red spider mite.

Primula acaulis
syn Primula vulgaris
(Primulaceae)
Primrose

Essentially this is the common primrose, but it has been developed by plant breeders in recent years to produce plants of great beauty in an exciting range of wonderful colours. They are quite hardy, and are excellent for chilly places in the home which need brightening up. Colours range from rich reds, yellows, oranges, rose pink, cream and white, and often there is a contrasting vivid yellow 'eye'. A primrose in the home reminds us of early morning walks in spring,

when the sight of a wild primrose inspires hopes of release from the dismal days of winter. The name literally means 'first rose' and there are many affectionate folk terms for the wild flower. It is called Butter rose and Lent rose in Devon, Darling of April, Early rose, Easter rose, Golden rose and Golden stars in Somerset. In the language of flowers, the meaning attributed is 'early youth'.
As a house plant, the primrose likes cool, light and airy conditions.

Care

Temperature
10°–18°C (50°–65°F) Day
  4°–10°C (40°–50°F) Night

Position: Anywhere cool and light.

Watering: Water every day when in flower.

Feeding: Feeding is not necessary.

Extra care: After flowering the plant can be placed in the garden.

Flowering time: Late winter and spring. About two weeks.

Cineraria cruenta
syn Senecio cruentus
(Compositae)

A group of these rainbow coloured little pot plants is well worth buying for the sheer drama of their impact. They are available in a riot of colours, which glow like jewels. Choose from reds, pinks, purples, blues, white, with contrasts from coloured centres or contrasting petal edges. The flowers are daisy like, and provide instant cheer. The plant originates from the Canary Islands, and is usually available between early winter and spring. They remain in flower for about six weeks, and require cool conditions and plenty to drink, also some humidity.
The cultivars sold are from the **'Starlet'** strain.

Care

Temperature
7°–10°C (45°–50°F) Day and Night

Position: Either in good light or a little shade, but never in direct sunlight. Avoid draughts.

Watering: These plants drink a lot, so keep the compost moist all the time.

Feeding: Feeding is not necessary.

Extra care: Watch carefully for greenfly. Discard after flowering.

Flowering time: For six weeks, between early winter through spring.

Guzmania lingulata
(Bromeliaceae)
Scarlet star

Guzmania is an extremely attractive and unusual houseplant, and is a typical bromeliad, found in the rain forests of Central and South America. The plant is epiphytic in habit, and lives in the forks or on the branches of trees. It is a rosette forming plant, and the central leaves overlap to form a water holding vase which the plant uses to collect rainwater in the wild. Thus it gets food and water through the vase whilst the roots are used to anchor the plant. The flowers rise from the centre of the plant, and are surrounded by brightly coloured bracts. The cultivar sold, *G. lingulata* **'Minor'**, bears a spike of scarlet, yellow or orange bracts, surrounding yellowish flowers. The plant is about 30cm (12in) high, and the rosette is about 20–30cm (12–18in) across. The leathery strap like leaves have purple markings. The plant flowers in winter and the bracts stay colourful for some months.

Care

Temperature
21°–22°C (70°–72°F) Day
16°–18°C (60°–65°F) Night

Position: Place in good natural light, but protect from direct sunlight. Keep away from draughts.

Watering: Do not overwater. The plant grows best if it is kept slightly dry.
The central vase can be kept filled with soft tepid water, rather than wetting the compost.

Extra care: The plant flowers only once, but the following year it will produce new growth at soil level from which flowers will appear for the following year.

Flowering time: Flowers appear in winter, bracts last several months afterwards.

Exacum affine
(Gentianaceae)
Arabian violet, Persian violet

This is a charming compact little plant with a bushy habit, and shining deep green leaves which are rather oval in shape. The plant usually grows about 15cm (6in) high, and bears delicate, saucer like flowers. These are lavender blue with yellow stamens, and have a pretty fragrance. The flowers are about 12mm ($\frac{1}{2}$in) across, and bloom from June to November. *Exacum* is found wild in the Gulf of Aden and Socotra, and the cultivar usually used for pot plants is **'Midget'**. The plant needs warm conditions with plenty of light.

Care

Temperature
18°–21°C (65°–70°F) Day
16°–18°C (60°–65°F) Night

Position: Place in maximum natural light, out of direct sunlight. Avoid draughts and chills.

Water: Keep the compost moist at all times.

Feeding: Feed once a week from June onwards until the flowers are over.

Extra care: Remove dead flowers. Discard the plant after it has finished flowering.

Flowering time: Continuously from June to November.

Rosa chinensis minima
(Rosaceae)
Pot rose, miniature rose

These are exquisite miniature roses which are available in flower from early spring through autumn depending on the variety. The plants are exact but tiny replicas of the garden roses, and it is as if an Alice in Wonderland transformation has occurred. They

Left: *Rosa chinensis minima.* **Right:** *Exacum affine.* **Centre: The dramatic and unusual** *Guzmania lingulata* or Scarlet Star.

are even pruned with nail scissors! Most pot roses grow about 15–30cm (6–12in) high, and *R. chinensis minima* is the basic parent of many cultivars which are achieved by cross breeding. The most popular rose is undoubtedly the red bloom, and this is the colour sold by Marks and Spencer, chosen, no doubt, to express its direct meaning in the language of flowers – 'I love you'. Although they look very delicate, pot roses are in fact quite hardy, and it is important that they are

kept cool in winter, to become completely dormant during the resting period.

Care

Temperature
20°–22°C (68°–72°F) Day
10°–18°C (50°–65°F) Night

Position A good light position while in flower, a few hours direct sunlight will be beneficial.

Watering: Keep roots fairly moist, but do not overwater. Decrease watering in the winter, but do not allow the roots to dry out.

Feeding: Feed once a week with good quality plant food from early summer, until flowering ends.

Extra care: Remove dead flowers regularly, and keep watch for greenfly and mildew. After flowering the plant can either be placed out in the garden or in the coolest part of the house to overwinter. In late winter cut back the shoots to promote new growth. Start watering again in the spring, and feeding from early summer. Repot if necessary in general purpose potting medium.

Flowering time: Four to six weeks after purchase.

Euphorbia pulcherrima
(Euphorbiaceae)
Poinsettia

This must be one of the most popular plants for Christmas, and although it comes from Mexico, it has now joined the holly and the ivy as familiar members of the indoor flora for the festive season. The plant is mainly grown for its showy leaf bracts, which surround the tiny yellow flowers in the centre of the stem. The leaves are lobed and a pretty bright green, contrasting well with the bracts. Most poinsettias are specially bred in compact form, and grow about 30–60cm (1–2ft) high, and with luck, the plants can remain attractive for four to six weeks. They need lots of humidity and steady warmth.

Care

Temperature
20°–22°C (68°–72°F) Day
18°–20°C (65°–68°F) Night

Position: Place in maximum natural light, out of direct sunlight, and out of draughts.

Watering: Water frequently, and never let the compost dry out.

Feeding: Feed once a week.

Extra care: To ensure you get the best flowering time, provide lots of humidity by standing the plant in a tray lined with pebbles and filled with water, or else putting the pot into a larger container lined with peat which can be kept constantly moist. Spraying the bracts will also help. The plant is usually discarded after the leaves and bracts fall.

Flowering time: From four to six weeks after purchase.

Jasminum polyanthum
(Oleaceae)
Chinese jasmine

To walk into a room which has a jasmine pot plant growing there can be pure delight, for this is one of the most deliciously scented of all indoor plants. The white starry flowers are pink when they are in bud, and cover the plant profusely during the winter months. The plants can survive at comparatively low temperatures, but they should not be allowed to get too chilled or they are liable to lose their foliage. This jasmine variety comes from China, and is a semi-evergreen climber. It has dark green divided leaves about 7.5–12.5cm (3.5in) long which are composed of five to seven leaflets. The flowers are about 2cm (¾in) across and are borne in clusters from January through to April.

Care

Temperature
20°22°C (68°–72°F) Day
10°–13°C (50°–55°F) Night

Position: Jasmine requires a light, sunny position. A few hours direct sunlight will be beneficial.

Watering: Water frequently

during periods of rapid growth, but do not allow the plant to become waterlogged. Water sparingly at other times, but do not allow the compost to dry out. Use tepid water.

Feeding: When new growth appears, feed once a week with a good quality plant food. Do not feed during the resting period.

Extra care: After flowering is over, prune back the flowering shoots. New shoots will appear the following year. Maintain a humid atmosphere, and spray plant often. Watch for red spider mite especially in dry atmospheres.

Flowering time: Four to six weeks after purchase.

Schlumbergera gaertneri syn Rhipsalidopsis gaertneri
(Cactaceae)
Easter cactus

This is a pretty flowering cactus from Brazil which produces its blossoms in the spring. It is epiphytic in habit, which means that it perches on the branches or in the forks of trees. It is also described as a 'link-leaf' cactus, which refers to the manner in which it produces its flat, succulent leaf like stems. New stems grow out of the end of the preceding one, sometimes in pairs. These appear after the flower has died down. The stems are about 5cm (2in) long, and have regular notches. At the end of the line of links grow the pretty flowers, which are starry shaped and scarlet. They appear from April onwards, and bloom for about eight weeks.

Care

Temperature
21°–24°C (70°–75°F) Day
10°–18°C (60°–65°F) Night

Position: Keep in maximum natural light, but out of direct sunlight. Protect from draughts.

Watering: Water when the compost feels dry, and do not allow the plant to stand in excess water in the pot holder.

Feeding: Do not feed while the flowers are in bloom.

Extra care: After the flowers are finished, allow the plant to go nearly dry. When active growth starts again, water regularly and feed once a week. A dry period is necessary during October and November to promote flowering. Restart watering when the buds emerge.

Zygocactus truncatus syn Schlumbergera truncata
(Cactaceae)
Christmas cactus, Crab cactus.

Like the Easter cactus, see previous entry, the Christmas cactus is epiphytic in habit, and also comes from Brazil. It produces its leaf stems and flowers in the same manner. The stems are bright green with red markings. They are very deeply notched and resemble crab's claws, hence one of their common names. The flowers are distinctly tubular, rather like fuchsias, and bloom

earlier than the Easter cactus, appearing during the winter months. Individual flowers last three to four days, and appear singly from the end of the stem.

Care

Temperature
20°–21°C (68°–70°F) Day
16°–20°C (60°–68°F) Night

Position: Place in maximum light, out of direct sunlight and protected from draughts.

Watering: Water when the compost is slightly dry, and do not allow the plant to stand in excess water in the potholder.

Feeding: Do not feed while the plant is flowering.

Extra care: After flowering is over allow the plant to go nearly dry. When active growth starts again, water regularly and feed once a week. A dry cool period during July and August is necessary to promote flowering. Maintain a temperature of 13°C (55°F). Restart watering when the buds emerge.

Flowering time: For three to four weeks during the winter.

Below: *Schlumbergera gaertneri*

Small is
Beautiful

St Michael

SMALL FOLIAGE
PLANTS

Hedera
(Araliaceae)
Ivy

Helix is the Latin term for a snail or a screw. This is descriptive of the twining habit of the ivy stem. The local folk names for *H. helix*, the common ivy from which most cultivars are derived are also fascinating. Scottish names include Bentwood, Bindwood and Hibbin, while an old Leicestershire name, Lovestone, refers to its habit of climbing over stone walls.

Ivy was traditionally endowed with protective powers, and was wreathed with holly at Christmas to act as a potent combination against bad spirits. Farmers used ivy to protect milk, butter and dairy animals, and the plant was also used medicinally. Drinking from a cup carved from ivy wood was believed to cure whooping cough, a poultice made from the leaves was used to treat abscesses, and a vinegar made from the berries was in widespread use during the great plague of London. Ivy may have been one of the earliest houseplants, possibly in the homes of the ancient Romans and Greeks – it was almost certainly used as a plant for pots in their courtyards. It was often used to make garlands and wreaths for festivals, and it has strong associations with the god Bacchus, at whose celebrations the image was crowned with an ivy chaplet. Modern cultivars are the most useful of all foliage plants for the home. They are quite hardy, and excellent for chilly spots, as well as situations where the light may be poor. This makes them especially valuable, because it is often difficult to find plants suited to such situations. The ivies are very useful for beginners, as they are not very demanding, and are generally easy to grow. They can be grown as climbers, trailers, sometimes in bushy form, and have a wide range of pleasing leaf shapes and variegations. The varieties sold include the following cultivars:

H. helix **'Pittsburgh'** This vigorous grower has small, dark green leaves with lighter green veins. The leaf shape is roughly triangular, though in fact it has five lobes. Fully grown, the leaf is about 3cm (1¼in) long and 2.5cm (1in) wide.

H.helix **'Chicago'** This is similar to **'Pittsburgh'**, though the leaves are larger, about 5cm (2in) long and 3.7cm (1½in) broad. Young leaves are bright green, and stay light green in maturity.

H. helix **'Harald'** This is a variegated sport from **'Chicago'**, and the variegation occurs on the leaf margin. The young leaf is deep cream, turning to ivory as the plant matures, while the centre of the leaf is mottled in grey and green.

H. helix **'Glacier'** An attractive cultivar with a silvery grey effect, **'Glacier'** has light and dark green leaves with creamy yellow patches, mostly around the leaf edges. The stems have a pretty purple tint.

H. helix **'Eva'** Often known as **'Little Eva'** this cultivar has leaves which change colour as they age. When young, the leaves are almost entirely ivory, but as the plant matures, the leaves become mottled in dark and light green, starting from the centre. The leaf has three lobes, and grows in varying shapes.

Care

Temperature
15°–18°C (60°65°F) Day
10°–13°C (50°–55°F) Night

Position: As already mentioned, *hedera* can tolerate a wide variety of light and temperature conditions. However, it should not be placed in direct sunlight, or in strong draughts. In winter it will thrive happily in an unheated room, and prefers cool conditions generally.

Watering: Water when the compost is quite dry. Add tepid water slowly until it drains into the pot holder, and do not allow the plant to stand in excess water.

Feeding: Feed once a week from April to September with a good quality plant food.

Extra care: Ivy attracts dust, and its health and appearance can be improved by sponging or spraying the leaves with tepid water. Keep growth in check by cutting back unwanted growth. This can be done at any time.

Watch carefully for scale insects, which can cover the foliage with a black, sticky secretion. Control of scale insects is described on page 21, however the plant can be placed outdoors for a time in winter, as frost is most effective in killing off this pest. Fortunately, ivy will tolerate a short period of frost, though it might shed its leaves. These will grow again in the spring.

Nephrolepis exaltata
(Oleandraceae)
Ladder fern

Also commonly known as the Sword fern, the genus is named from a combination of two Greek words, *nephros* meaning kidney, and *lepis* a scale. This describes the kidney shape of the spore sacs on the underside of the leaves. *N. exaltata* was one of the most popular ferns in Victorian households, where they were mainly displayed in hanging baskets. The fern has returned to deserved popularity, and the variety sold, **'Bostoniensis'** has attained great acclaim in America. Modern breeding methods in England have further enhanced its quality and consistency. They use a 'cloning' method by which the tissues from a selected mother plant are placed on a special agar medium taken from seaweed. This operation is performed in a bacteria-free laboratory, and one tissue in a test tube produces five plants within days. When these are split and placed in larger containers, the same happens again. This system ensures that only the finest specimens are reproduced.

In the wild, *N. exaltata* grows in damp, shady places in tropical conditions – they are found all over the West Indies. It may even have been brought to England by the

Above left: Two specimens of the versatile *Hedera*. **Right**: The beautiful *Nephrolepis* fern requires extra humidity if it is to thrive (see extra care).

famous Captain Bligh, of *'Mutiny on the Bounty'* fame. He was responsible for the first large-scale introduction of tropical ferns into the country. After his voyage on the Bounty failed, he made another trip to the West Indies on the *Providence*, and brought back a large collection of plants for the Royal gardens at Kew, including 37 species of ferns.

N.e. **'Bostoniensis'** is often called the Boston fern, and has elegantly cascading fronds up to 1m (3ft) in length. These have a characteristic herringbone pattern creating arching, graceful foliage. They look superb in a hanging basket or on a pedestal, where their fronds are free to cascade.

Care

Temperature
20°–22°C (68°–72°F) Day
13°–16°C (55°–60°F) Night

Position: This fern thrives best in indirect or filtered natural light, in a position well protected from draughts. They can also tolerate a slight amount of shade. The temperature must never be allowed to fall below 10°C (50°F) in the winter. If only artificial light is available, supply eight to ten hours daily.

Watering: Water frequently in summer, more sparingly in winter. The soil should be kept barely moist at all times. To water, add tepid water slowly until it drains into the pot holder, and do not allow the plant to stand in excess water.

Feeding: A liquid feed of nitrogen high fertilizer once a week from April to September will ensure the growth of new fronds.

Extra care: Humidity is very important to the health of this plant, combined with steady warmth. To improve humidity, the pot can be placed in a larger container which is packed with peat. This should be kept damp at all times. It also helps to spray the fronds with tepid water in summer. If you notice that any frond is growing to a different shape from the rest, remove it entirely, as the plant will possibly revert to type. This is unlikely to happen in 'cloned' plants however. Pot bound plants should be repotted in early spring. Use a combination of potting soil and moss peat or leaf mould in equal parts.
(N.B. *Nephrolepis* is also sold in a medium size).

Grafted cacti 'Strawberry' and 'Banana'.

Gymnocalycium Mihanovichii Optum Rubra
Strawberry Grafted Cactus

Chamaecereus Silvestrii Lutea
Banana Grafted Cactus

These extraordinary little plants are called grafted cacti because a coloured variety, which has lost much of the chlorophyll, which gives plants their green colour, is grafted onto a green rootstock. The rootstock for the **'Strawberry'** and **'Banana'** is *Selenicereus Grandiflora*. The **'Strawberry'** originally comes from Japan, whilst the **'Banana'** originates in Brazil. In appearance they resemble a red ball and a bunch of bananas growing on top of a prickly, fleshy green cylinder.
They make an attractive display when grouped together in twos and threes.

Care

Temperature
10°–27°C (50°–80°F) Day
6°–10°C (42°–50°F) Night

Position: In summer keep in a hot, south facing aspect with full sunlight. In winter grafted cacti should be kept in good light.

Watering: Water thoroughly but allow compost to almost dry out before re-watering. Reduce watering from September stopping altogether in mid-October until mid-February when the plant can be sprayed two or three times a week. By the end of the month give a little water to the roots.

Feeding: Feed with a high potash type of fertiliser (as used for tomatoes). One third to one half strength will encourage growth. Do not feed from mid-August until April.

Extra care: There is no extra care for grafted cacti.

Adiantum raddianum syn. A. cuneatum
(Polypodicaceae)
Maidenhair fern

If you plunge a frond of this dainty fern in water, you will see that the leaflets are covered with a layer of silvery bubbles. *Adiantos* is the Greek word for 'dry' and refers to the fern's characteristic impermeability to water on the leaf surface. *Adiantum* is a native of Brazil, and would not be instantly recognizable as a fern, with its rounded leaflets and thin, wiry stems. The clue to its fern identity is the presence of clusters of raised brown spots on the undersides of the leaves of adult plants. These are the little sacs containing the fern spores.
The cultivar sold is called *A. cuneatum* **'Fragrantissimum'**. A common name for *A. cuneatum* is 'delta fern' and the **'Fragrantissimum'** variety has sweet smelling fronds up to 30cm (1ft) in length.
The plant is really delightful, with its clouds of small, round leaflets growing across its glossy, black wire-like stems. It can reach a height of 50cm (20in) and is easy to care for.
N.B. Varieties sold in stores are labelled *Adiantum fragrans*.

Care

Temperature
16°–21°C (60°–70°F) Day
13°–16°C (55°–60°F) Night

Position: Like all ferns, the Maidenhair dislikes direct sunlight, but needs good natural light and generally warm conditions. It should be guarded from draughts.

Watering: Keep the compost moist during the summer months, but water sparingly in winter – just enough to keep the frond from wilting. Never allow the compost to dry out completely. The plant should be watered at the base with soft, tepid water.

Feeding: During the growing period (April to September), the plant should be fed weekly with a dilute solution of plant food.

Extra care: Humidity is vital to the health of the fern, and can be supplied in the same way as for *Nephrolepis*, see page 43. Without sufficient humidity the leaflets turn brown at the edges. The best winter temperature is about 10°C (50°F). The plant cannot tolerate frost, and in low temperatures it can suffer badly. Repotting can be done in spring, using a limefree growing medium. Make sure that the rhizomes are on the compost surface, and not buried.

Two examples of *Dracaena* 'Red Edge', with a Maidenhair fern, *Adiantum raddianum*, (**Front**).

Dracaena terminalis 'Red Edge'

(Liliaceae)
Dragon Plant, ribbon plant

The dracaena is also known as a cordyline which name comes from the Greek word for a club as the leaves appear to be club shaped. In *D.* **'Red Edge'** the leaves are edged and tinged with a glowing cerise colour when young. As the plant matures, this changes to a bronze coloured centre with a cerise edge. Leaves are about 12.5cm (5in) long by 37mm (1½in) wide.

Care

Temperature
18°–27°C (65°–78°F) Day

16°–21°C (60°–70°F) Night

Position: Place in a warm bright position but keep out of direct sunlight. Avoid draughts and chills.

Watering: Keep the compost well moistened by thorough and regular watering using tepid water. During hot dry weather, more water is required but do not overwater and do not let the plant stand in excess water.

Feeding: Feed once a week from April to September with a good quality plant food.

Extra care: Mist occasionally with tepid water to supply extra humidity. The plant maintains and develops its colour best when it is kept in a bright light.

Room to
Grow

St Michael

MEDIUM FOLIAGE
PLANTS

Monstera deliciosa
(Araceae)
Swiss Cheese plant, Mexican bread fruit.

Despite its need for moderate warmth all year round, this species has become a very popular houseplant in recent years. It does best in centrally heated homes with reasonable humidity, and needs to be supported on stakes to allow it to climb freely as it does in its native Mexico. The plant is often seen gracing the reception areas of offices, where its size creates great impact. The literal meaning of its botanical name is 'delicious monster' and refers not only to its dimensions but also to the taste of its fruit, which looks like an elongated pale green pineapple, and tastes like a mixture of banana and pineapple.

The leaves are very large and round shaped, even on young plants. On fully grown plants they can become enormous, tending to elongate to 1m (3½ft). In a conservatory the plant can reach at least 3m (10ft) and much taller in its native habitat, where it climbs up the trunks of trees and eventually emerges into daylight. The leaves are curiously slashed and in mature plants they become elongated holes rather than slits. Their colour is a pleasing medium green, with a glossy sheen. Mature plants produce large arum like flowers, usually in groups of two or three and these appear at any time of the year. The spathe of the flower is creamy yellow, and the interior surface has a fine diamond like pattern impressed over the entire area. The large central spadix develops into the fruit, which unfortunately has a fibrous texture. Do not allow children to eat the fruit as the fibres can stick on the tongue and in the throat. The plant sends out long aerial roots. In its native habitat these penetrate the moss growing on tree trunks and use it to climb, but in pots, they may turn downwards and enter the compost, travelling a long distance.

The best way to grow *Monstera* is up a moss covered stake. The support must be firm, with at least 5cm (2in) covering of sphagnum moss, mixed with a little bonemeal and secured around the stake with wire. *Monstera* is a greedy feeder, and the bonemeal will provide extra nourishment for the aerial roots as they penetrate the moss. Since the plant can grow very tall, it can be kept in check by cutting off the top. This encourages the formation of sideshoots.

This species can survive at temperatures as low as 7°C (45°F) but it is risky, especially in the case of a large plant which may deteriorate. Ideally a minimum temperature of 18°C (65°F) should be maintained, to encourage rapid growth, which may be inconvenient in a confined space.

Care

Temperature
24°–27°C (75°–80°F) Day
18°–21°C (65°–70°F) Night

Position: Place in good natural light but out of direct sunlight. The plant will tolerate a certain amount of shade, though this will mean that the leaves will stay relatively small.

Watering: *Monstera* must have plenty of water at all times, unless the minimum temperature has to be maintained in winter. Watering should then be cautious, and the roots kept slightly dry. Since the plant likes humidity, the moss surrounding the stake should be kept well soaked.

Feeding: Feed once a week from April to September with a good quality plant food.

Extra care: The foliage responds very well to treatment with a leaf shine preparation, taking on a brilliant gloss. Repotting should be done in spring, using a peat based compost. The plant is rarely troubled by pests, but low temperatures, erratic watering and low humidity cause the leaves to yellow and develop brown patches. The occasional unsightly aerial root may be removed without harm.

Caladium bicolor
(Araceae)
Angel's wings

The leaves of this beautiful plant really do look like angel's wings, not only because of their shape, but also due to their delicate paper thin texture. They can grow as large as 50cm (20in) long, and are bred into all kinds of exquisite colour combinations. The native habitat

of the plant is the jungle region of Brazil and the Amazon. Caladiums require extra care in home conditions. The temperature should never be allowed to fall below 13°C (55°F), and they also need a high degree of humidity, which can be provided by standing them on pebble lined trays filled with water, or else standing them in a larger container lined with damp peat. They can also be grouped with other warmth and moisture loving plants to create a self contained micro-climate. Misting the leaves in the summer with a very fine mist, using tepid water will also aid humidity. The caladium is not evergreen, and the leaves die down in autumn, duplicating the plant's resting habit in its natural environment. The roots are tuberous and edible

Two beautiful examples of *Caladium bicolor* (front) with a glossy Monstera.

(in the tropics they are known as cocoa roots), although eating your houseplants is not recommended. The following cultivars are sold:
'Candidum' The leaves are pale, whitish green with darker green veining, making a delicate tracery.
'White Christmas' Almost identical to *'Candidum'*.
'Freda Hemple' The leaf has a brilliant red centre which is margined in green. The outline of the leaf is slightly wavy.
'Rosebud' The leaf has a pink centre with pink veins, shading out to a network of yellow markings, and a light green leaf margin.
'Kathleen' Beautiful, soft pink leaves, with a wash effect just like an Impressionist painting. The veins are red, and the pink tinge blushes out into a green margin.

Care

Temperature
18°–24°C (65°–75°F) Day
12°–18°C (60°–65°F) Night

Position: Provide good natural light, but not direct sunlight because the leaves are very fragile and can easily burn. Be careful to protect from draughts.

Watering: In summer the plant drinks quite a lot, water when the compost is fairly dry. As the leaves die down, reduce the water, till you are supplying just enough to keep the compost barely dry.

Feeding: Feed once a week from April to September with a good quality plant food.

Extra care: Some people prefer to remove the tubers from the pot after the leaves die down. If you do this, let the soil dry out, knock the plant out of the pot, and shake off the soil. Trim off the dead tops, and treat the tubers with a combination of fungicide and insecticide. They are best stored in dry peat or vermiculite, at 13°–16°C (55°–60°F). Store about four to five months, then repot in peat compost.

Dieffenbachia picta
(Araceae)
Dumb cane, Leopard lily, Mother-in-law plant.

The genus was named after Herr Dieffenbach who was gardener at the Imperial palace in Vienna during the 1830s. The plant is native to Central and South America, and thrives in warm, moist conditions which means that it must have plenty of humidity. *Dieffenbachia* is a very popular houseplant, and much prized for its handsome foliage. It is rather fussy about its environment however, and unless it receives adequate warmth all year round, in a draught-free position, it can deteriorate. When conditions become too cool it will retaliate by dropping its leaves.

All parts of the plants are poisonous, because it contains calcium oxalate, which irritates the mouth and throat if any part is eaten. The effect is so unpleasant that the plant is popularly called 'Dumb cane' because it is reputed to cause temporary loss of speech. This is also the reason why some people (thinking wishfully perhaps?) call it by its common name, the Mother-in-law plant.

The sap from the leaves of this plant may irritate the mouth and throat if eaten. Keep out of the reach of children!

The leaves are large, oval to spear-shaped, and very handsome and dramatic in appearance. There are four cultivars sold:

D.p. **'Exotica Perfecta'** is a fine robust looking plant with ivory markings on the leaves. The veins and margins are green.

D.p. **'Compacta'** is similar, but has bushier growth due to its habit of throwing out side shoots from the base of the plant.

D.p. **'Marianne'** is bred from 'Exotica Perfecta' with the result that an overall whiter tinge to the leaf is achieved.

D.p. **'Camilla'** is bred from **'Compacta'** again to produce an overall white tinge to the leaf with a bushy habit similar to **'Compacta'**.

Care

Temperature
21°–27°C (75°–80°F) Day
18°–21°C (65°–70°F) Night

Position: Give the plant a very bright position in winter, but shade slightly in the summer months. Although it is found in quite windy conditions in the wild, it hates draughts as a pot plant.

Watering: Water carefully. The compost must not stay wet for long periods. Add tepid water only when the compost feels dry.

Feeding: Feed once a week between April and September with a good quality plant food.

Extra care: As the plant likes lots of humidity, it can be stood on a pebble lined tray filled with water, or placed in a larger peat lined container, so that the peat can be kept moist. Another method is to group it with other moisture loving plants to create a micro-climate. Spray the leaves occasionally with tepid water, and repot in spring using a good general purpose potting medium.

Dracaena marginata syn Cordyline marginata
(Liliaceae)
Madagascar Dragon Tree

This is a very attractive houseplant which looks like a small, multicoloured palm tree. The cultivar sold is called **'Tricolor'** and is a quite recent introduction. The plant is usually bought when it is about 30cm (1ft) high, and although it is very slow growing, it can eventually reach about 1.5m (5ft) *D.marginata* **'Tricolor'** has a slender central trunk which supports a large rosette of narrow leaves, drooping over in typical and elegant palm fashion. the leaves are about 37cm (15in) long, and about 2cm ($\frac{3}{4}$in) wide, beautifully variegated in cream and green stripes with reddish margins. *Dracaenas* derive their species name from the Greek word for dragon, and grow in a large variety of shapes and sizes. Species are found in the tropical regions of India and Africa, and the plant needs plenty of warmth and humidity to thrive.

Care

Temperature
21°–24°C (70°–75°F) Day
18°–21°C (65°–70°F) Night

Position: Place in a good, strong natural light, but not in direct sunlight. Protect carefully from any draughts and chills.

Watering: Keep the soil moist in summer, but rather dryer in winter. Use tepid water, and never let the roots stand in excess water left in the potholder.

Feeding: Feed once a week from April to September with a good quality plant food.

Extra care: Since this plant needs lots of humidity, either stand it in a tray lined with pebbles and filled with water, or place the container in a larger one lined with peat which can be kept moist. Spray the leaves in summer. When repotting becomes necessary, use a loam based potting medium.

Cordyline terminalis
syn Dracaena terminalis
(Liliaceae)
Cabbage palms

Also sold as *Dracaenas* are the plants known more accurately as *Cordylines*. The name comes from the Greek word for a club, and is an apt description for the shape of the leaves which are often about 30cm (1ft) long and about 10cm (4in) across. These are houseplants of remarkable beauty, and are usually sold when they are about 45cm (1½ft) high, but can reach heights between 1.5–15m (5–10ft). These varieties are used in their native habitat in Polynesia as the source of supply for roof thatching materials and also the fabric for exotic hula skirts. Please do not ransack your unsuspecting plant when you can't think of what to wear for the fancy dress party. The hula skirt leaves come from somewhat maturer specimens. Typical houseplant varieties are about 30–90cm (1–3ft) tall, with a slender trunk, and leaves growing from the top. These are stunningly attractive – the cultivars sold are:

'Prince Albert' which has a deep cerise pink at the leaf centre, shading out to purple-brown, flecked with red.

'Lord Robertson' has a dark red leaf beautifully marked with pink stripes.

'Atom' has fiery red colouring all over the leaf. The coloured leaf forms of *Cordylines* were brought back to England from the South Sea Islands by James Gould Veitch in 1866. They require excellent warmth and humidity.

Care

Temperature
24°–27°C (75°–80°F) Day
18°–21°C (65°–70°F) Night

Position: Place in the brightest light possible, some direct sunlight will not harm the plant, but this should not be constant. Avoid draughts and chills.

Watering: Keep well moistened in summer, but barely moist in winter. Do not let the plant stand in excess water.

Feeding: Feed once a week from April to September with a good quality plant food.

Extra care: Supply humidity as for *D. marginata*. The plant can be pruned if necessary. Repot in general purpose potting medium.

Left: Dracaena. **Centre:** Dieffenbachia. **Right:** *Cordyline terminalis.*

Schefflera actinophylla
(Araliaceae)
Heptapleurum, Umbrella Tree,
Green rays

The genus was named after the
Danzig botanist J.C. Sheffler, and is
native to Indonesia, northern
Australia and New Zealand. It is
also sometimes called the Octopus
tree, due to the shape of its scarlet
flowers which only grow when the
plant is in its wild habitat. The
genus is composed of small trees or
shrubs, which can grow very tall,
and the variety sold, *S. arboricola*
is nicely compact and shrubbier in
its habit than other kinds. The
plant produces dark, glossy green
leaflets shaped like spears. In
young specimens, there are about
three, and as the plant matures it
can produce groups of about six or
seven. These leaflets grow from the
tops of the stems, and make the
umbrella formation that explains
one of its common names.
The plant is quite happy at 10°C
(50°F) minimum temperature, and
is therefore suitable for fairly cool
environments. It will tolerate a
certain amount of shade (shade not
gloom) though it needs reasonable
light during winter.

Care

Temperature
18°–24°C (65°–75°F) Day
13°–18°C (55°–65°F) Night

Position: *Schefflera* grows best
when it is in a light, airy position,
but as previously noted, it can
stand some shade. The plants
should be kept out of draughts and
direct sunlight, otherwise some
leaf drop might occur.

Watering: Between April and
September, keep the compost
moderately dry between thorough
waterings. During winter keep the
compost barely dry.

Feeding: Feed once a week
between April and September with
a good quality plant food.

Extra care: The winter minimum

Above left: Schefflera arboricola.
Right: Chamaedorea elegans.

temperature has already been
mentioned, but avoid raising the
temperature over 16°C (60°F)
during this period, otherwise the
plant will try to grow when it
should be resting, and becomes
weakened. It can then be more
prone to infestations with scale
insects. In summer, try to provide
some humidity, and sponge the
leaves occasionally with tepid
water. Potting on should be done in
the spring with a loam based
potting compost, and the plant kept
moist at all times until it is settled.

Chamaedorea elegans
syn. Neanthe elegans
(Palmae)
Parlour palm.

Also known as the dwarf mountain
palm, *C. elegans* is a native of
Mexico. Although it is seen in its
fullest glory as a mature, graceful
palm, when young it is frequently
used in dish gardens and
terrariums, since it seems quite
content to live in these cramped
conditions. In its natural habitat it
grows in the shade of taller trees,
so this might explain its
accommodating nature at an early
age.

C. elegans belongs to the palm family, and grows to about 1.2m (4ft) tall. It has fine, narrow leaves and arching stems and fronds, producing a graceful, slightly languid drooping effect. It makes an excellent accent plant amongst modern settings. Individual leaves are about 13cm (5in) in length, and are pinnate i.e. feathery in appearance. The fronds vary, but are usually about 30cm (12in) long. A mature parlour palm might produce flowers, these are yellow plumes along the flower stem, and after they are over, shiny little fruits follow. This usually occurs in very hot and humid summers. It is one of the easier palms to grow.

Care

Temperature
20°–22°C (68°–72°F) Day
12°–14°C (53°–58°F) Night

Position: This palm likes good, strong natural light, but not direct sunlight which might damage its leaves. It dislikes draughts, so keep it sheltered.

Watering: Water freely in summer, and keep the compost well moistened. In winter it needs less moisture, but do not allow the compost to dry out. Use tepid water, the softest available.

Feeding: Feed once a week between April to September with a good quality plant food.

Extra care: A regular spraying with tepid water during the summer months will be much appreciated. Moderate temperatures are adequate, but winter temperatures should never exceed 12°–14°C (53°–58°F). Repot only when the roots are very crowded and new growth is retarded, using a peat based compost plus extra sand.
N.B. The Parlour palm is also sold as a small size specimen. The care for that size is as given here.

Yucca elephantipes
(Liliaceae)
Spineless Yucca

The yucca is becoming increasingly popular as a houseplant, and comes from Central America and the south of the U.S.A. The plant is an evergreen shrub which has a palm like look, though it in fact belongs to the lily family. Yucca is often bought as a miniature 'tree' for indoor use, but it can grow up to 4.5m (15ft) high, making a very dramatic and unusual accent plant. A young specimen has a sturdy little trunk from which baby leaflets can be seen emerging in the growing season. The foliage is comprised of tufts of dark green spear shaped

Far left, centre: The exotic and dramatic Yucca Elephantipes. **Right:** *Ficus elastica* or Rubber plant.

leaves which have rather rough edges. When the yucca is mature the leaves are about 50cm (20in) long, and droop from the trunk rather like the foliage of a giant pineapple. Large specimens need to

spot. Yucca can be put outside on the porch or patio in good summers, but never let them be exposed to frosts. Young specimens are best kept indoors until they have been potted on to tubs and are well established. They do best in winter temperatures of around 7°C (45°F).

Watering: Water just enough to keep the growing medium barely damp during the summer. In winter the plant should be kept very slightly moist.

Feeding: During the growing period, April to September, feed once a week with a good quality plant food.

Extra care: Yucca will need to be repotted to accommodate its increasing size. Pot on when the roots look crowded, using a proprietary compost.

Ficus elastica
(Moraceae)
Rubber plant, Fig

A native of tropical east Asia. *F. elastica* can grow as high as 35m (100ft) in the wild. The tree was originally tapped for its rubber, the source of all those squashy erasers which bring back such immediate memories of schooldays. The tree now used for commercial rubber extraction is *Hevea brasiliensis* which belongs to the spurge family. The variety used as a house plant grows on a single stem, which reaches about 1.2m (4ft) and has glossy dark green leathery leaves which are large and dramatic. This is the plant most frequently given by women to their menfolk – it is thought to have a definite 'masculine' appeal.
The cultivar sold is *F. elastica* 'Robusta'. Its leaves can grow very large, up to 44cm (18in) long and 22cm (9in) wide. The midrib of the leaf is reddish on the underside, and the growing tip at the top of the plant is enclosed in a red-tinged sheath. When new growth proceeds, the sheath splits open and falls away to reveal the new

leaf. The plant is surprisingly resilient to low temperatures, and also to fumes from oil and gas. However, this should not encourage you to neglect your rubber plant, since it responds magnificently to good conditions and care.
If there is any plant which can be said to represent the modern equivalent to the Victorian aspidistra, this must certainly be the prime candidate.

Care

Temperature
21°–24°C (70°–75°F) Day
18°–21°C (65°–70°F) Night

Position: Place in a good natural light, but out of direct sunlight. When new growth occurs, move the plant to a slightly shadier position so that the leaves can expand more fully. The rubber plant dislikes draughts more than variations in temperature, so keep it sheltered.

Watering: Overwatering causes the leaves to turn yellow, and since they are so thick and leathery, the damage will have been done by the time you notice the symptoms. In the summer, just keep the compost moist, and be especially careful in the winter not to overwater when the plant is resting. It is at this time that the most damage is likely.

Feeding: Feed once a week from April to September with a good quality plant food.

Extra care: The leaves should be carefully sponged clean with tepid water at regular intervals, since the large surface area can harbour dust. The leaves also respond beautifully to cleaning with a good leaf shine preparation.
Do not be too eager to repot, since the plant does best in a small container, even if the roots do get a little overcrowded. A 60cm (2ft) specimen will be happy in a 13cm (5in) pot, and repotting needs only to be done every two or three years, when new leaf growth seems to be stunted. Then you can repot using a general purpose potting compost.

be grown in tubs and the plant generally likes lots of sunlight.

Care

Temperature
10°–21°C (50°–70°F) Day
7°–10°C (45°–50°F) Night

Position: Place in a warm sunny

Big,
Bold and
Dramatic

St Michael

LARGE FOLIAGE
PLANTS

Fatsia japonica syn. Aralia sieboldii
(Araliaceae)
False castor oil plant, Fig leaf palm.

Fatsia is the phonetic English equivalent of the Japanese name for the plant, and has nothing to do with its being overweight! The plant is native to Japan and Taiwan, and has been a consistently popular houseplant for well over a century and a half. Despite its ability to tolerate frost, the leaves look somewhat tropical. They have a typical palmate shape, consisting of seven to nine lobes cut deeply into attractive shapes. It makes a fine, impressive plant for a porch or entrance hall, provided there is reasonable light. *Fatsia* is almost hardy in habit, but it will suffer badly in prolonged cold conditions. In autumn it produces white flowers which gradually expand into an umbrella-like spray, which last for several weeks and are followed by black berries.
In the wild it is an evergreen shrub, and can exceed 3m (10ft) in height. It is slow-growing however, and its height indoors will normally be about 1.2m (4ft).

Care

Temperature
10°–18°C (50°–65°F) Day
 4°–13°C (40°–55°F) Night

Position: As mentioned previously, this is a hardy little plant and all it needs is plenty of light.

Watering: The compost needs to be kept reasonably moist in summer, and should be watered just enough to prevent drying out in the winter months when it is resting.

Feeding: Feed once a week during April to September with a good quality plant food.

Extra care: The leaves can be sponged with tepid water, or cleaned with a leaf shine preparation. Keep the plant in relatively small pots until it becomes overcrowded, then transfer it to 20cm (8in) pots, using a general purpose compost. After the flowers are finished, remove the heads by pinching them off back to the nearest leaf.

Ficus benjamina
(Moraceae)
Weeping fig

A member of the same genus as *F. elastica*, the rubber plant, *F. benjamina* is another extremely popular houseplant which has brought much pleasure to indoor gardeners for many generations. The plant has shiny, pointed, leathery textured leaves 5–10cm (2–4in) in length, which grow from gracefully arching branches, giving the distinct 'weeping' effect. It is usually grown to produce trees about 1.2–1.8m (4–6ft) high. *F. benjamina* can sometimes react dramatically when moved too abruptly from one location to another, especially if there is a drastic reduction in the light source. When the plant is newly introduced to the home, it should be provided with similar light to its in store environment, and should never be put in shade.

Care

Temperature
21°–24°C (70°–75°F) Day
18°–21°C (65°–70°F) Night

Position: The plant does best in bright natural light, or, if artificial light is used, this should be for about ten hours daily. The plant dislikes draughts and shade.

Watering: Keep barely moist at all times, and only provide water when the compost appears dry, adding tepid water very slowly until it drains into the pot holder. Remove excess water from the holder.

Feeding: Feed once a week from April to September with a good quality plant food.

Extra care: Sponge the leaves with tepid water to preserve their gloss, or use a leaf shine preparation. As with *F. elastica*, do not repot too often, because the plant does well in fairly small pots. Only repot when the new leaves seem stunted. Repot in spring, with a general purpose potting compost.

Citrus mitis
(Rutaceae)
Calamondin orange, Miniature orange tree

There is a special enchantment about this delightful little tree, and many people are tempted to grow miniature citrus plants from pips. These often grow too large, and their production of fruit may be erratic, so this trustworthy specimen is well worth purchasing. Oranges have always been regarded as useful in a variety of ways, as well as having romantic associations with the traditional bride and her head garland of orange blossom. The oil expressed from the seed is used to flavour many products, and is also an important ingredient in good quality Eau de Cologne. Orange trees are quite hardy, but they need more heat and sun in summer.than the notorious British climate can provide. *C. mitis* originates from the Philippines, and makes a lovely houseplant. It will grow to about 30–45cm (1–1½ft). It is a bushy evergreen, producing fragrant white blossoms in the spring, continuing at intervals until the autumn. The miniature fruits are about 3.5cm (1½in) across. The flowers are plentiful and very pretty. It is quite common for a plant to bear fruit and flowers simultaneously, in late summer, with some individual fruits continuing to change colour throughout the winter and into the following spring. The fruits are small and green when first seen. Then they ripen into perfect oranges about the size of a walnut.

Care

Temperature
20°–22°C (68°–72°F) Day
10°–13°C (50°–55°F) Night

Position: Though the plant can be placed outside in a very hot summer, to ensure optimum conditions it needs to be placed in a very warm bright spot indoors. A sunny window ledge is ideal.

Watering: Water with care since the roots are temperamental and need excellent drainage. Keep the compost fairly moist, but do not give too much water in summer. In winter supply just enough to keep the compost barely dry.

Feeding: Feed twice a week from April to September with a good quality plant food.

General care: If the flowers are to set, good humidity must be provided, either with a pebble lined tray filled with water, or a larger container lined with damp peat. Spray the flowers overhead with a fine mist of water. Do not repot too often, as the roots dislike being disturbed. Use a loam based compost, and repot in spring. Any pruning should be done in spring to prevent the plant from becoming straggly or leggy.

Chrysalidocarpus lutescens
(Palmae)
Areca palm, Butterfly palm.

This graceful member of the palm family comes from Mauritius and the tropics. Its delicate feathery foliage is composed of long, narrow pinnate leaflets growing from the branches in a fan-shape. At full maturity it reaches 6m (20ft), but is usually seen as a houseplant when it is very young, growing around 1.2–2.5m (4–8ft) tall. The stems and leaves have an attractive yellow tinge. New leaves are delicately joined at the tips, giving a fascinating tracery effect while the leaves are growing. The fronds are quite long, about 90cm (3ft) on an average size plant, and the stems of older specimens are marked with rings where old leaf growth occurred.

Care

Temperature
21°–27°C (70°–80°F) Day
18°–21°C (65°–70°F) Night

Position: This adaptable palm grows best in bright natural sunlight, but out of direct rays. Avoid placing it in draughts.

Watering: The soil should be kept moist at all times, and the roots should never be allowed to stand in excess water in the pot holder. Water less frequently during the winter months.

Feeding: Feed once a week from April to September with a good quality plant food.

Extra care: Repotting may be necessary, and should be done in spring using a general purpose potting medium. Once the plant has grown too large for indoors, it can be moved outside in frost free conditions.

Rhoicissus rhomboidea
(Vitidaceae)
Grape ivy, Natal ivy

A native of Natal in South Africa, *R. rhomboidea* makes an attractive climbing plant for shady places in the home. It has shiny dark green foliage, composed of groups of three diamond-shaped, irregularly edged leaflets. In the young stage, the leaves and shoots are covered in brown hairs. The plant will reach at least 1.5m (5ft) if allowed, and can be grown even taller.

Care

Temperature
13°–18°C (55°–65°F) Day
10°–13°C (50°–55°F) Night

Position: The plant tolerates shade or a north facing position. It also manages well in bright natural light, and enjoys plenty of fresh air in summer.

Watering: Water when the compost seems dry, but avoid overwatering. In winter, keep the compost barely moist.

Feeding: Feed once a week from April to September with a good quality plant food.

Extra care: The leaves should be sprayed with tepid water during the summer months, and supplied

The amenable *Rhoicissus rhomboidea* or Grape ivy accompanied by two beautiful examples of *Chrysalidocarpus lutescens* or Areca palm.

with reasonable humidity, Pinch off stem tips if a bushier growth is required, though the plant will still need to be supported on a stake. Repot in spring, but do not use peat based compost – it prefers a soil based potting medium.

Howea syn. Kentia Palm
(Forsteriana)

The palms favoured by the palm court orchestras of cafés and tea rooms were probably of this species of Howea. The Kentia Palm originated in the Lord Howe Islands where it can grow up to 18m (60ft) tall in the wild. It is not difficult to grow and care for and is probably the tallest and most graceful palm that can be grown under container conditions. The Kentia is distinguished by its long, slender, upward arching leaflets which give it a feathery appearance, and has a thick cuticle and waxy covering which help prevent moisture escaping.

Care

Temperature
13°–21°C (55°–70°F) Day
10°–18°C (50°–65°F) Night

Position: Place in natural daylight but out of direct sunlight. Protect from draughts.

Watering: Water when the compost is slightly dry. Add tepid water slowly until it drains into the pot-holder.

Feeding: Feed once a week from April to September with a good quality plant food.

Extra care: Keep the atmosphere fairly moist by occasionally misting with tepid water.

Yucca Tips
(Liliaceae)
Spineless Yucca

This dramatic plant, is merely a part of the Yucca elephantipes which is sold in the medium foliage range. It grows, and needs to be cared for in exactly the same way, as it is just the top of the tree. For care see page 55.

Left: Yucca tips and Kentia palm.

The Perfect Combination

Trailing Plants and Arrangements

Among the most popular of Marks and Spencer's selection of houseplants are the trailing plants and special arrangements. These range from bottle gardens which are sold at Christmas and for Mother's Day, to attractive hanging pots and arrangements presented in pottery bowls, wicker baskets and terracotta troughs. The presentation will vary from time to time, but in the main, flowering arrangements are presented in small and large plastic bowls, wicker squares and oblongs, posy baskets and mixed baskets. Green arrangements come in small and large pottery bowls, and terracotta troughs and bowls. Trailing plants are sold in discreet green hanging pots with detachable hooks, and pot holders. The selection of plants in each arrangement may vary from season to season depending on availability, but all the plants in the arrangements are selected for their visual and growth compatibility. In addition to those plants with individual entries in the next few pages, Marks and Spencer sell trailing varieties of plants which have been covered in detail elsewhere.
These include *Pelargonium pelatum*, ivy leaf geranium (see page 28), *Fuchsia* (see page 32) and *Campanula isophylla*, Italian bellflower (see page 32).

Tradescantia
Wandering Jew, Inch plant

This most attractive trailing plant is named after John Tradescant, a plant collector, and gardener to Charles I. It originates from South America, but was first introduced into Europe during the seventeenth century. Marks and Spencer sell two varieties, *Tradescantia* **'Silver Queen'** which has white-striped, pale green leaves and *Tradescantia* **'Tricolor'** which has delicately white-striped pale green leaves

with pink edges. **'Silver Queen'** has slightly more robust leaves.

Care

Temperature
10°–21°C (50°–70°F) Day
7°–13°C (45°–55°F) Night

Position: To maintain the variegated leaves keep in bright light but out of direct sunlight.

Watering: Water when the compost is slightly dry. Add tepid water slowly until it drains into the pot-holder. Do not allow the plant to stand in excess water.

Feeding: Feed once a week from April to September with a good quality plant food.

Extra care: Tradescantia enjoy humidity, so mist from time to time with tepid water.

Impatiens sultanii
Busy Lizzie

This very popular flowering plant makes a particularly useful trailing plant which can be grown out of doors after danger from frosts has passed. The **'Busy Lizzie'** cultivar favoured by Marks and Spencer is Futura and all plants sold are varieties of this cultivar, and come in a range of colours. How the Impatiens came by its common name is not known, but it is possible that it derives from its prolific growing and flowering habit. In the right conditions it will flower almost throughout the year, constantly sending out new shoots and extending those already present. However **'Busy Lizzie'** is almost as famous for dropping its flowers as it is for producing them. The fleshy stems and rapid growth indicate a plant which needs regular and fairly frequent watering and which enjoys humidity. If its flowers do drop it is probably because the atmosphere or compost is too dry.

Impatiens really prefers not to be in centrally heated conditions and dislikes being moved too often.

Care

Temperature
10°–21°C (50°–70°F) Day
7°–10°C (45°–50°F) Night

Position: Place the plant in maximum natural light but keep out of direct sunlight.

Watering: Keep the compost moist with thorough and regular watering using tepid water. During hot, dry weather more water is required.

Feeding: Feed once a week, from April to September, with a good quality plant food.

Extra care: Allow the plant some air on really hot days and protect from too dry an atmosphere. Remove any dead flowers.

Chlorophytum capense syn. C. elatum; C. comosum
(Liliaceae)
Spider plant, St. Bernard's Lily

The Spider plant, which comes from South Africa, must be one of the most frequently purchased houseplants. Yet it is not often seen at its best, since many people neglect it, and do not appreciate its true beauty. The foliage is long, narrow, arching and rush like. There are two main forms of variegation – either with a creamy white band down the leaf centre, or a green centre with creamy margins. *Chlorophytum* may be very much a favourite with your pet cat, especially if access to the garden is not available. Many feline friends take frequent 'snacks' on the leaves of the plant, which may explain why so many have untidy leaf edges. To deter your pet from this habit, grow it in a tray of budgerigar seed, or move the chlorophytum to a safe place. When grown and cared for properly, the Spider plant will produce luxuriant, gleaming foliage, and during summer, long stems will arise from the leafy clumps and bear tiny white starry flowers. These stems can reach 75cm (2ft) in length, and among the flowers small plantlets – exact replicas of the mother plant – are formed. These ultimately weigh down the stems to give a gorgeous cascading effect. In the wild, they reach down to the soil and take root, but if you leave them, they will cling to the stems for years, growing in size.

Care

Temperature: 7°–13°C (45°–55°F) Day and Night

Position: The plant needs good light, but should be kept out of direct sunlight. Make sure it has plenty of room to grow and cascade downwards, either in a hanging basket, on pedestals, room dividers etc. Draughty conditions may cause the leaves to turn yellow or brown.

Watering: Water enough to keep the compost well moistened in summer, but just enough to prevent the roots from drying out in the winter months.

Feeding: Feed once a week from April to September with a good quality plant food. If the leaves turn brown, this can also be because of inadequate feeding.

Extra care: Provide good humid conditions for the best foliage growth, and repot in spring using a general purpose potting medium.

Above left and **centre left:** *Campanula Isophylla,* Italian bellflower **Centre:** *Impatiens sultanii,* Busy Lizzie **Below right:** *Scindapsus aureus* **Bottom:** *Rhoicissus Rhomboidea* 'Ellen Danica'.

Rhoicissus rhomboidea
(Vitidaceae)
'Ellen Danica'

This cultivar is especially suitable for hanging and trailing purposes. The main genus is discussed on page 60, and the only extra care information needed for **'Ellen Danica'** is to control excess growth by pruning back the stems in winter. New growth will occur in the spring.
'Ellen Danica' has distinctly serrated leaf margins compared to those of the main genus.

Care

Position: The plant tolerates shade or a north facing position. It also manages well in bright natural light, and enjoys plenty of fresh air in summer.

Watering: Water when the compost seems dry, but avoid overwatering. In winter, keep the compost barely moist.

Feeding: Feed once a week from April to September with a good quality plant food.

Extra care: The leaves should be sprayed with tepid water during the summer months, and supplied with reasonable humidity. Pinch off stem tips if a bushier growth is required, though the plant will still need to be supported on a stake. Repot in spring. Do not use peat based compost – it prefers a soil based potting medium.

Scindapsus aureus
(Araceae)
Devil's ivy

A genus of climbing plants from the Solomon Islands, *S. aureus* is effective as a trailing plant. It is also a climber. It is now called *Epipreminum aureum* by botanists. It has broadly spear-shaped leaves but as the plant matures, they become more heart-shaped, and the plant produces smaller leaves.

One of the cultivars sold is **'Marble Queen'** which has white markings on the leaves, giving a striking 'netted' effect. The other variety sold is called *S. pictus argyraeus* often called the Silver vine. The leaves are even more distinctly heart-shaped than *S. aureus*, and are quite small, about 5cm (2in) long. They are olive green dotted with silver.

Care

Temperature
21°–27°C (70°–80°F) Day
14°–18°C (58°–65°F) Night

Position: Place in slight shade, but not too much, since the leaves of *S. aureus* will revert to plain green. Avoid placing in draughts.

Watering: Keep the compost well moistened during the summer months, but water less frequently during the winter.

Feeding: Feed once a week from April to September.

Extra care: Both cultivars need humidity, and should also be sprayed regularly in summer. *S. pictus* is particularly sensitive to chills, and should be well protected. To avoid straggly growth, remove leading shoots late in winter. Repotting is best done in spring, using a peatbased compost with some granular charcoal added. If plants grow too large, prune drastically in June.

Plants for Arrangements

The majority of plants used in arrangements have been discussed elsewhere individually. Marks and Spencer select from a wide range of flowering and green plants for their arrangements. The precise content of each will vary with the seasonability of the plants, but the following list represents the range of choice. *Adiantum cuneatum* **'Fragrantissimum'** (see page 44), *Chamaedora elegans* (see page 52), *Chlorophytum capense* (see page 66), *Dieffenbachia picta*

'Camilla', **'Exotica'** and **'Marianne'** (see page 50), *Dracaena marginata* and **'Red Edge'** (see page 45), *Euonymus japonicus* (see page 73), *Hedera* varieties (see page 42), *Euphorbia pulcherrima* (see page 38), *Azalea simsii* (see page 26), *Kalanchoë blossfeldiana* (see page 28), *Chrysanthemum* (see page 35), *Cyclamen persicum* (see page 34),

Begonia (see page 27), *Cineraria cruenta* (see page 36), *Pteris ensiformes* (see page 70), *Nephrolepis exaltata* (see page 42–3), *Rhoicissus rhomboidea* (see page 60), *Scindapsus aureus* and *Scindapsus* **'Marble Queen'** (see page 68), *Cissus antarctica*, commonly known as the Kangaroo vine is also included in green arrangements. This is very similar in habit to *Rhoicissus rhomboidea* (see page 60). *Cissus antarctica's* leaves have distinct, red, hairy petioles. A very attractive variety of ivy that is not listed amongst the main hedera often used in arrangements is *Hedera helix canariensis*, commonly known as the **'Canary Island Ivy'**. The cultivar used is called **'Gloire de Marengo'**. This has very attractive large leaves with dark green centres, shading silvery-grey to a white margin. Several plants used in the arrangements will need further detailed description.

A selection of arrangements available at different times during the year. The varieties of plants may vary from season to season.

X Fatshedera lizei
(Araliaceae)
Fat-headed Lizzie, Ivy tree

The sign ×denotes a hybrid, in this case bi-generic (using two genus plants). *F. lizei* was created by crossing *Fatsia japonica* **'Moseri'** with *Hedera helix* **'Hibernica'**. The resulting plant can best be described as a shrubby climber. The hybrid was produced in 1912 by Lizé brothers at their nurseries in Nantes, and is an immensely successful houseplant. It has attractive shiny 3–5 lobed leaves about 5cm (2in) wide. Like *Fatsia japonica* it is quite hardy and easy to grow, and can be made quite bushy by judicious pruning in spring.

Peperomia
(Piperaceae)

There are about 1,000 species in this genus, which usually have very strong, succulent leaves. Most *peperomias* come from the forests of South America and the West Indies, and have a nice compact habit. Two varieties are sold. *Peperomia magnoliaefolia* **'U.S.A.'** has thick green leaves with yellow markings. Some peperomias have really unusual 'quilted' leaves, and the other variety included in green arrangements, *Peperomia caperata* **'Emerald Ripple'** is a very beautiful example of these types, with a strong contrast achieved by dark and lighter green shading on the leaves.

Pteris ensiformis
(Pteridaceae)
Silver Lace Fern

The genus name was used by the Greek physician Dioscorides, and is derived from the Greek word for a feather, which refers to the frond shape. The variety sold is called **'Evergemensis'**, and is a very attractive Belgian cultivar.

The plant is small in habit with good, firm fronds. These grow in clusters and are attractively variegated with white stripes on the main vein and down each pinna. The other variety of *Pteris* sold is *Pteris cretica* **'Wimsettii'**, which has distinctive 'tassels' on the ends of the leaflets.

Maranta leuconeura
(Marantaceae)
Prayer plant, Rabbit's tracks

Maranta is a lovely foliage plant, and has the endearing habit of closing its leaves to an erect position in darkness, just like hands held in prayer (hence one of its common names). *M. leuconeura* is also called **'Rabbit's tracks'** because of the bold spots arranged symmetrically along each side of the central leaf vein. These spots also give it another common name, the 'Domino plant'. Most varieties come from Brazil, where they grow in forest clearings. The leaves have a very distinctive herringbone pattern, and the main cultivar sold is *M. l. erythrophylla*, or more commonly *Maranta* **'Tricolor'**. The oval leaves are usually held more erect than other forms, and are richly coloured in dark green with red veins and a yellow midrib. The entire leaf may have a red tint.

Pilea cadierei
(Urticaceae)
Aluminium plant

This plant was originally discovered in the forests of Vietnam, and was introduced to France in 1938. It is the parent plant of all further cultivars. Its common name is given because of the somewhat metallic sheen on the white markings on the leaves as if they were literally painted with liquid aluminum. *Pilea* in fact belongs to the nettle family, and the other variety sold, *Pilea mollis*, commonly known as the Moon Valley plant, certainly is

more reminiscent of its family origins. *P. mollis* comes from Mexico and has distinctly nettle shaped leaves with a hairy surface. The surface of the leaf is deeply quilted and the contrast pattern is created by the dark and light green colours making a relief pattern on the surface.

Syngonium podophyllum
(Araceae)
Goosefoot plant

Podophyllum indicates that the leaves are shaped like a foot – in this case a goose foot. This is a very attractive plant, which originates from Central America, and is evergreen and climbing in habit. The cultivar sold is called **'White Butterfly'**, and the leaves are roughly triangular in shape, rather like an arrow head. They are shiny white in colour, with green margins. The leaves change their shape and colour as they grow. They divide up into several leaflets and eventually become entirely green when the plant is fully mature.

Asparagus plumosus syn. A. setaceus
(Liliaceae)
Asparagus fern

Gerard and Culpeper ascribed to the plant they knew as Sperage or Sparrow grass the properties of increasing seed and stirring up lust! They were of course referring to the edible variety, not the ornamental fern that we know, and it cannot therefore be promised that your innocent houseplant can supply such excitement.
To complicate the issue even further, *A. plumosus* is not a fern at all – it belongs to the lily family. Though this may seem wildly unlikely, if you examine the flower under a microscope, it will be evident that the flower is very like a bluebell, which certainly does belong to the lily

family. *A. plumosus* is grown for its exquisite, delicate foliage, which is often used by florists to set off bouquets of cut flowers. The leaflets are in fact like little needles, and they grow from wire-like stems in the form of graceful, feathery fronds. The original form is erect and neat in the early stages, and throws out trailing stems when mature. The plant may produce scarlet berries.

Arrangement in a bottle garden.

Hypoestes sanguinolenta
Spotted dog, polka dot plant

This pretty spotted plant makes a most attractive splash of colour in a green arrangement. Originally from Madagascar, its foliage is spotted with pink. In bright light the colour intensifies, whilst in poor light the spots may shade to white. Extra care should be taken to avoid burning the leaves which are rather thin, whilst providing good daylight to maintain the colour.
If the leaves do burn you can identify the problem as large brown patches will appear on the leaves and they will become papery. Remove damaged leaves and turn the arrangement so that the plant is protected.

Care of arrangements

As previously mentioned, arrangements are composed of plants which are naturally complementary in terms of their preference for similar growing conditions. They also provide each other with a good microclimate which helps to maintain healthy growth. General care is the same for all the arrangements.

Position: The arrangement should be placed in a warm, draught free position in good natural light, but out of direct sun. Variegated plants must face light source.

Watering: Keep the compost moist with regular and thorough watering. Use tepid water, and supply extra during hot weather. Do not overwater however, just keep the compost moist all the time.

Above: A selection of plants for the bottle garden arrangements.

Feeding: Feed once a week from April to September with a good quality plant food.

Extra care: Spray occasionally with tepid water, and keep leaves of green plants clean and shining, either by sponging with tepid water, or with leaf shine where appropriate.

Plants for Bottle Gardens

Ficus radicans

(Moraceae)
Rooting fig, Trailing fig

This is yet another member of the genus *ficus* which includes the Rubber plant (page 55) and the Weeping fig (page 58). What is it doing in the bottle garden? The answer in short is that it is providing a good source of 'wandering' greenery which makes useful ground cover, and adds to the 'jungly' effect. The plant roots from its stems, and thrives well in the humid climate inside the bottle. The leaves are narrow and leathery in texture, and are about 5cm (2in) long with slender points. They have a healthy, glossy foliage, sometimes variegated with cream edges.

Hoya carnosa

(Asclepiadaceae)
Wax plant

The plants which do best in the bottle garden are usually foliage varieties, and it is therefore very pleasing to find a suitable flower to add to the collection. Hoya comes from Queensland in Australia, and the cultivar used is *H. variegata*. The plant produces delightful clusters of pale pink starry flowers during May to September. These have red star shaped centres, and a delicate fragrance. In the language of flowers, the wax plant means 'susceptibility', and one can leave it to the individual imagination to decide what the basis of susceptibility is. An extra bonus of the plant is found in its very attractive leaves. These are blue green with red shading and creamy white edges. The plant therefore serves a dual purpose in the bottle garden, providing lovely flowers and foliage at the same time. Hoya was named after Thomas Hoy who was gardener to the Duke of Northumberland.

Vriesea splendens

(Bromeliaceae)
Flaming Sword

This is an absolutely stunning plant, providing dramatic impact in the bottle garden. It is a bromeliad, which means that it consists of a rosette of leaves spraying out from a central crown at ground level. The leaves grow around each other to make a vertical tube before they fan out, and the plant uses this tube to collect rain water. Unlike most plants, the roots are not so important, they are merely used to anchor the plants securely. Most bromeliads are found growing on other plants, they are epiphytic in habit, and are found in the jungle forests of Central and South America. *Vriesea splendens* takes its name from W. H. de Vriese, a Dutch botanist, and has beautiful leaves cross banded in a dark purple brown. The vivid flower head represents the 'flaming sword', and is thrust up from the rosette of leaves. The head is composed of brilliant red overlapping bracts which contain the tiny yellow flowers inside. The flowers appear in mid to late summer, and often last for about two months.

Euonymus japonicus

(Celastraceae)
Spindle tree

Although the variety found in the bottle garden is a native of Japan, it is interesting to note that we have our own native Spindle tree. This has always been known for the use made of its wood – it has been made into pegs, skewers, toothpicks, anything in fact which requires a tough, hard wood. Local names abound, but a few examples will suffice. Pegwood, Skiver tree (Devon), Skewer wood (Dorset, Wiltshire), Spindle wood (Gloucestershire) and more ominously, the fruits were called Louseberries, since they were baked and powdered to sprinkle on children's hair to delouse them. The forms used in the bottle garden are compact varieties, *Euonymus japonicus* 'Aurea', and 'Microphyllus'. The leaves of both are basically spoon shaped and slightly serrated. The 'Aurea' variety has the larger leaf, which has a pretty golden sheen, and the 'Microphyllus' variety is smaller. The name means 'your charms are engraven on my heart'.

Cryptanthus

(Bromeliaceae)
Earth Star

This is another bromeliad, but unlike the *Vriesea*, it is usually found on the ground, rather than perched on a tree. The cultivar in the bottle garden is called 'Tricolor', which has leaves striped in creamy yellow and green, tinted pink from the centre which makes a welcome splash of colour in the green arrangement.

Care of bottle gardens

Position: Place the arrangement in good natural light but not in direct sunlight, otherwise the glass will act as an intensifying medium for the sunlight.

Watering: Be careful not to overwater the arrangement. Water only when the compost becomes dry. A certain amount of natural humidity is retained in the bottle, and too much watering will encourage rotting and fungus.

Feeding: Feeding is not necessary.

Extra care: If any of the plants grow too vigorously and start to smother the others, pruning will be necessary. Use a pair of nail scissors. The opening at the top of the bottle will allow you to put you hand inside. Special tools are available for tending the bottle garden but a kitchen fork extended with a stick is sufficient.

Inside
Out

St Michael

BULBS, CORMS
& TUBERS

Bulbs, corms and tubers

In addition to supplying houseplants already planted up in pots, Marks and Spencer also offer an excellent range of bulbs, corms and tubers which you can cultivate yourself. These either come in packets, or in kit form (a growing container and potting medium is sold with the bulbs). Many people are not aware of the differences between bulbs, corms and tubers, and it would be useful to clarify exactly what these are.

Basically, they are all storage organs produced by the plants in different ways in order to provide food for the following year.

A bulb is in fact a complete plant in itself, but in embryonic form. If you cut a bulb vertically down its centre, you can identify the different parts. The bottom of the bulb holds the base-plate, which is the plant's main food storage area. From it grow the roots and the leaves. Right at the centre of the bulb is a tiny stalk, which holds the flower spike surrounded by minute scales. As the plant grows, the spike thrusts upwards, and the scales enlarge into leaves. In fact all the enlarged scales forming layers in the bulb are modified leaves, and help in the process of food storage. Once growth is well under way, the bulb shrinks, because its food is being used up, however when the plant is above ground and carrying out photosynthesis, it starts returning food back to the bulb in preparation for its next dormant period, and the following growing season. The time when the bulb naturally flowers depends on its country of origin, though some are specially treated to allow them to be 'forced' into flower for Christmas and the New Year.

Corms are the swollen stem bases of a plant, and like bulbs, these also have a base-plate which produces the roots and the top growth. The central 'bud' is much smaller in comparison with that of a bulb, and while bulbs renew themselves annually, the corm dies at the end of each year, while the nutrients formed during flowering are used to create a brand new corm. A gladiolus corm is typical of this process. However some corm producing plants, such as varieties of begonia, behave differently. The corm does not die, but increases in size (bulbs return to their original size) and after several seasons, these enlarged corms will have to be divided into segments, each with its own growing tip.

Tubers are another form of storage organ, but unlike bulbs and corms, they are modified stems which carry buds. There is no base-plate, and the nutrients are stored within the tuber for the following year's growth. Dahlias and some varieties of begonias have tuber storage organs.

Cultivating bulbs

All the bulbs supplied are spring flowering, except for the hippeastrum cultivars which are specially treated for early flowering, and also hyacinths, which are similarly prepared for forcing. The crocus is often mistaken for a bulb, when it is in fact a corm, but as it is also spring flowering, it can be conveniently included with bulbs. As previously mentioned, the bulbs are presented in different ways. The kit packs are designed for indoor early flowering bulbs, and include hippeastrum amaryllis, hyacinth and crocus varieties. In addition, there are two hyacinth cultivars which are sold in packets, but are also treated for forcing purposes. These are not supplied with pot and compost, you must plant them yourself. All the other bulbs are suitable for bedding purposes, and can be planted outside. They flower later than the specially treated bulbs, according to their natural growth cycle. These include narcissi/daffodils, tulips, snowdrops, also two varieties of 'untreated' hyacinths.

Growing indoor bulbs

The only difference between the kit-packed bulbs and the specially treated hyacinths is that you have to supply your own pot and bulb fibre for the latter. Otherwise the growing procedures are exactly the same. Place some bulb fibre in the pot, and insert your bulb or bulbs if you are planting several, with the pointed end up. Do not push the bulbs down harshly, just nestle them into the surface. The bulbs should then be covered and given a thorough watering. They now need a period of darkness and cool conditions. A cupboard would be ideal, but make sure that the temperature is around 5°–9°C

Below: Amaryllis 'Striped'.

(40°–48°F). Leave them for the period recommended, which will be between six to twelve weeks. Check them every two weeks to make sure that the fibre is adequately moist. If the fibre dries within the first two weeks, the temperature is too high. As soon as the tips appear they should be yellowish green. Now they need to be moved out of the dark, but not into too much heat – 10°C (50°F) is ideal. Once buds are showing, move the bulbs to a warmer place and maintain a temperature of 16°C (60°F) or even a few degrees higher. Now the bulbs have the chance to burst into their full glory. While flowering they should be given maximum light, and the bulb fibre needs to be kept moist at all times.

The varieties of early flowering bulbs for indoors are as follows: Crocus **'Remembrance'** (deep blue). Hyacinth **'Delft blue'**; **'Pink Pearl'**; **'Carnegie'** (white). Amaryllis **'Apple Blossom'** (pale pink); **'Red Lion'** (flame red); **'Striped'** (orange with white stripes).

Growing bulbs outdoors

If you have a garden, you already have the ideal setting for cultivating your outdoor bulbs. You simply plant at the recommended time and nature does the rest. You may be more interested in the design aspect of cultivation – should you plant lots of the same kind together? where do they look best? should you mix up different kinds? Park keepers plant bulbs in large 'drifts' for example, and tend to keep the same variety in one area. Some people dislike the look of bulbs planted in any regimented manner, and prefer the softer effect of 'naturalized' planting, often in grass. By this method, you basically scatter the bulbs as they fall, and dig a small

Below left: Delicate Snowdrops 'Elwessii'. **Right:** Daffodils of the 'King Alfred' variety.
Bottom left: Deep blue Crocus 'Remembrance'. **Right:** The dramatic Tulips 'Kaufmanniana Stresa'.

hole for each. If you are planting in grass, you can buy a special tool which pulls out a plug of soil and grass making space for the bulb, which can then be topped with the plug. As for where to plant, the possibilities are endless – under trees, on awkward banks, in rockeries, and of course in containers such as window boxes. Remember however, that if you are planting in a container of any kind, it should have very good drainage, and the growing medium should be a good quality general purpose kind. The advantage of containers is that you can have bulbs blooming everywhere – on window ledges, on patios, down steps, wherever there is room for a pot or box in fact.

The varieties of spring flowering bulbs for growing outdoors are as follows:
Crocus **'Zwannenburg Bronze'** (purple); **'Snow Bunting'** (blue); **'Saturnus'** (white); **'Whitewell Purple'** (striped); **'Tomasianius'** (yellow).
Snowdrops **'Elwessii'**.
Hyacinths **'Lady Derby'** (pink); **'Carnegie'** (white); **'Delft Blue'**.
Daffodils/Narcissi **'King Alfred'** (yellow trumpet); **'Unsurpassable'** (large trumpet, deep yellow); Miniature yellow daffodil **'Tête à Tête'** (clear yellow with reflexed petals); **'Dutch Master'** (deep golden yellow, serrated trumpet); **'Verger'** (small trumpet); **'Carbineer'** (yellow petals, deep orange cup); **'Ice Follies'** (opens pale yellow, but becomes white); **'Cheerfulness'** (double variety with scented white and cream flowers, several to a stem).

Tulips **'Princess Irene'** (orange with a purple flush); **'Peach Blossom'** (deep rosy pink); **'West Point Lily'** (yellow); **'Burgundy Lace'** (wine red with frilled edge); **'Dreaming Maid'** (violet edged with white); **'Apeldoorn'** (orange-scarlet); **'Golden Apeldoorn'** (rich golden yellow); **'Kaufmanniana Red Riding Hood'** (attractive true red); **'Water Lily Tulip'** (creamy white with deep golden yellow bases and calmine on reverse); **'Clara Butt'** (pink).

Summer flowering range

A good selection of corms and tubers are supplied for planting out for summer flowering. Tuber producing varieties are dahlias and begonias, and the corm variety is the gladiolus.

Dahlias

Three kinds of decorative varieties are sold and two cactus types. The flowering season is from July to October, and the planting procedures are the same, depending on when you want to bring the plant into flower. For flowering from late August onwards, the tubers should be planted in the flowering position during late April to early May. For July/August flowering, the tubers should be planted up in pots or boxes in slightly heated conditions, during late February to early March. They can be hardened off in a cold frame out doors during April and planted out in May/June.

The soil chosen should be well drained and enriched with a good quality general fertilizer. Choose a good sunny position. Plant the tubers 10–12cm (4–5in) deep and 60–90cm (2–3ft) apart. The dahlias may need to be staked to support growth. Provide one stake per tuber when planting.

General care Water the tubers after planting, and during any dry weather. Protect from pests with slug bait and a good general

insecticide for aphid control. Remove dead flowers regularly. After flowering, allow foliage to die back, then cut the stem about 15cm (6in) above soil level before lifting the tuber. Store the tubers upside down in a cool, dry place protected from frosts. Replant the following year.

The following varieties are sold:
Decoratives 'Arabian Nights' (deep red with maroon red shading); **'Rosella'** (intense pink); **'Rocquencourt'** (orange); **'Promise'** (clear yellow) and finally the most attractive **'Park Princess'** (pink).

Above: Dahlias of the decorative variety.
Below: Begonias.

Begonias

Like dahlias, the bedding begonias can be planted at different times depending when you want to bring them into flower. For August flowering, plant in the growing position in late May. For July flowering, plant in boxes or pots in slightly heated conditions in late February to early March. Transplant out into the garden when danger from frost is over in late May–June.

The soil chosen should be well drained and enriched with a good quality general fertilizer. Plant in a sunny position. The tubers should be placed 7.5cm (3in) deep and 23–30cm (9–12in) apart. Make sure that the concave surface of the tuber is uppermost.

General care Follow the same care instructions as for dahlias. The variety sold is a double begonia in red, yellow and salmon.

Hanging begonias

The infinitely varied begonia family has lovely hanging types, which look pretty in window boxes or hanging baskets. The variety sold blooms from July to October. If you want to have flowers in August, you should plant the tubers in the flowering position in late May. For July flowering, plant the tubers in pots or boxes in slightly heated conditions during late February to early March. harden off in a cold frame during April, then plant in late May or early June when frosts are past. Choose a good quality general potting soil when planting into hanging containers and window boxes. Place the tubers in the soil about 7.5cm (3in) deep and about 13cm (5in) apart. Make sure the concave surface of the tuber is facing up.

General care: Make sure that the compost is kept moist, and feed once a week with a good quality fertilizer. At the first sign of frost, lift the plants, break off the stems, and clean tubers, Allow to dry completely, and store in a dry, cool frost-free place until replanting the following year.

The variety of hanging begonia sold is supplied in pink, red and yellow.

Gladiolus

The gladiolus corms flower from July to September. They can be planted from March to May, but the finest blooms are produced when the corm is planted as early as possible during this period. Plant in a good, well drained soil, enriched with fertilizer, and choose a sunny position. The corms should be planted 10cm (4in) deep and about 15cm (6in) apart. If you are growing them for cutting, you should double this distance between the plants however. The plants will need staking to support their growth. Stake when planting to avoid possible damage to the corm later on.

General care: Follow the same care instructions as for dahlias. See opposite page. The following varieties of gladiolus are sold:

'Flower Song' (clear yellow)
'Peter Pears' (soft orange)
'Ben Trovata' (rich pink)
'Oscar' (rich red)

Below: Gladiolus 'Peter Pears'.

Index

Acknowledgments

The Publishers would like to thank the following for their kind permission to reproduce the pictures in this book:
Geest 26 right, 38 left, 78 above; Harry Smith Horticultural Photographic Collection 26 centre, 33, 34 above, 36, 76, 77 above left, 77 below right, 78 below, 79; Spectrum Colour Library 77 below left; Michael Warren 73–74
Special Photography by: John Sims 20–23;
Theo Bergström Jacket, 1, 2–3, 4–5, 6–7, 10–11, 17, 19, 24–25, 27, 28, 29, 30–32, 34–35, 37, 38 right, 39, 40–41, 43, 45, 46–47, 48–49, 50–51, 53–72